from

Ancient Africa

Na'im Akbar, Ph.D.

MIND

PRODUCTIONS

Mind Productions & Associates, Inc.
324 N. Copeland Street
Tallahassee, Florida 32304

First Printing:	**July 1994**
Second Printing:	**March 1995**
Third Printing:	**June 1998**
Fourth Printing:	**March 2000**
Fifth Printing:	**April 2002**

Cover Design:	Malcolm Aaron
Backcover photo:	Michael Harris

Published by *Mind Productions & Associates, Inc.*
Tallahassee, FL 32304

Library of Congress Catalog Card Number: 94-96248
ISBN 0-935257-02-0

Dedication

My Mama, Bessie Weems King (Dec'd 1980)
My Aunt, Eunice S. Carter (Dec'd 1992)
My Daughter, Shaakira N. Akbar

FOREWORD

Light from Ancient Africa is another important block in the rebuilding of the African psyche; and the *"mind mason"* who has shaped and refined this block is my good friend and respected scholar, Na'im Akbar. I have known Na'im Akbar for over twenty-five years and I consider him to be one of the leading African psychologists in the world. His writings and teachings have helped to recenter Black psychology into its rightful African essence and foundation.

Because of my respect for Na'im's work, I am particularly honored to be asked to write the foreword to this new book. In a strange, if not mystical way, Na'im and my thinking and intellectual growth have progressed like twin steps along the same pathway. On many occasions, having not talked or heard from each other for a while, we would find ourselves at a conference, workshop or on a podium together, and after listening to each other's presentations, we would be startled that we had both reached the same place in our thinking or conceptualizations about some aspect of African psychology.

Over twenty years ago, Na'im and I, along with D. Phillip McGee and Cedric X (Syed Khatib), struggled to find the African voice in psychology. I don't think we knew then that we had set or been set upon a path that would lead to the reshaping of Black psychology as well as opening the gateway to the refinement of the notions of Africanity and Afrocentricity. For our part, the implication of this search for the African voice led to the simple yet awesome goal of liberating the African mind.

Light from Ancient Africa is a critical contribution to what might be called the *"Re-Africanization of Psychology Project."* It was within this project that we came to realize that the notion of human psychology was and remains an African invention. As such, and in order to make the discipline applicable to African people, one of the charges of contemporary Black psychology has been to define and refine an African psychology. In this book, Na'im Akbar provides the reader with a clear and concise understanding of the African (Kemetic) origins of psychology, provokes us to think deeply about the real meanings that Africa gave to psychology, and provides insightful *guidelines to modern day implications and applications of the field.*

*The discourse in **Light from Ancient Africa** is guided by Dr. Akbar's belief, which I also hold, that the utilization of the core ancient philosophical insights will help us to gain real and meaningful understandings of what has historically happened to African people and how we can change our condition from imperfect (disease) to more perfect (wellness). In discussing the "light" from Ancient Africa, Na'im rightfully focuses on Ancient Kemet (Egypt) and points out that ancient African conceptualizations of psychology can serve as important instruments in the liberation of the African mind. He notes, in this regard, as did Professor George G. M. James before him, that the light from Ancient Africa can and does serve as a source of mental emancipation from the prison of inferiority and dehumanization created by and reinforced with the distorted notions found in Western psychology.*

*The psychology of Ancient Kemet, nevertheless, remains to be rediscovered. In writing **Light from Ancient Africa**, Na'im Akbar has provided us with a carefully, albeit not perfectly, constructed blueprint for its discovery. In discussing the "Kemetic Origins of Psychology," Na'im points out that the wisdom of Ancient Kemet and the psychology that made it manifest was like a vast tapestry being defined by every other thread. Akbar further points out that no thread can be unraveled without destroying the entire tapestry. In effect, one must comprehend (think, feel, experience) like the Ancients in order to interpret and understand ancient ideas and beliefs. This is a critical and significant point. In reality, ancient Kemetic psychology cannot be understood with Western method (i.e., studying each component/thread separately). A full appreciation and understanding of ancient Kemetic psychology must be done with an African mind. This, of course, is the dilemma and the reason why the true sciences of Ancient Kemet remain essentially unknown. This is also why Black psychologists are the key to unlocking the mystery systems of Ancient Africa. We, (some) Black psychologists, are less blinded and less confused by the farce of Western psychology's hegemony and perpetration as being a universal or human psychology. We, accordingly, are more likely to explore seriously the path to discovering the authentic African spirit (Sakhu). In this regard, Dr. Akbar directs the reader to revisit all the threads of the African tapestry. However, the re-examination of fields like* *alchemy, astrology and numerology cannot be done without an African mind set. Even the profound notion that man is a microcosmic key to understanding the entire cosmos cannot be fully comprehended without an African mind.*

*Reading **Light from Ancient Africa** helps to regenerate the African mind. Dr. Akbar knowingly or maybe unknowingly stimulates our African consciousness by having us contemplate the use of African symbols, symbolism, metaphor and myth. The sheer act of contemplating the idea of Ba as the breath of the soul which enters into and activates the "being" of the person suggests a meaning of the person that is greater than one's physical existence. The Ba symbolized in a living form as a bird with a human head vibrating with energy that causes, I believe, a like vibration to resonate within our being. This African symbol, in effect, represents both the invisible and the visible and as such represents, as Akbar notes, the transmission of invisible energy through and to visible and living entities. Hence, the act of dealing with African concepts ignites and connects the invisible energy or spirit between the concept and us. At an esoteric level, the meaning of this symbol, accordingly, is capable of changing the meaning of ourselves. The potential of re-Africanization is hidden in the interaction with "things African." Each dimension of the soul, along with the metaphors and symbolism, found in the myths discussed in this powerful book need to be thought of in light of their transformative capacities.*

This directive is especially important in terms of Dr. Akbar's chapter on "Finding the African Self." While caution is necessary here, and the utilization of the African mind is required, the notion of "self" as essence is critical. Remember the tapestry. Contemplate the deeper symbolic meaning. Think with an African mind. Otherwise, you will miss what Akbar is saying.

What does Akbar mean when he says, "the Ba...is the original creative energy of the Creator and the Ba is the essence of the self?" What is the meaning of the symbolism of the heart? What is the deeper meaning of Ab (the word for heart) being a mirror reflection of the Ba? Why do traditional healers believe one must "touch the heart" in order to heal? What does it really mean to be "hard-hearted" or have a "heavy heart"? What does the Scarab mean, especially in terms of (re)generation, physical gender and the concept of masculine and feminine energy? Is there a deeper meaning? What does Akbar mean when he notes that nature or a divinely governed universe obeys strict order and that a unisexual culture will never fully build the African self?

Dr. Akbar notes that there is a relationship between the building of the Pyramids and what it takes to build the human spirit. What implication does this have for what we do as Black psychologists? He suggests that the building (via the union of spirit, soul, intelligence, energy and matter) of the Pyramids was psychology, not technology. In reading Akbar's chapter "Rameses II and Divine Kingship: A Spiritual Legacy," think deeply about the hidden meaning and its implication for our practice. What, for instance, is the meaning of god relative to the masculine principle? In speaking of the concept of Divine Kinship, Akbar notes that the Pharaoh was "god" not "the God" and functionally sought to systematically align his will with Divine will. Akbar further notes that the symbolism of the Pharaoh reflected the power of the strength of procreation and the importance of cultivating life through unity, peace, productivity and happiness of one's people. What is the meaning of Goddess relative to the feminine principle? Akbar notes that the Cobra Goddess represents vitality, concentration, precision and deadliness. She represents the power of psychology and the susceptibility of the mind. What does Akbar mean when he says the male and female must come together in "heart" as well as in body or that the female principle of energy must merge with the masculine principle of energy to procreate new societies, art, science and understanding? Think deeply about what this means. Does it inform the process of a Black awakening? What, if anything, does any of it have to do with therapeutic interventions or developmental strategies?

*In following our twin steps along the same pathway to the reclamation and re-ascension of African psychology, Na'im and I arrived almost simultaneously at the concept of Sakhu. As explained in this book, Sakhu means the understanding, the illuminator, the eye and the soul of the being, that which inspires. In effect, it is study, mastery and understanding of the process of human illumination. The Metu Neter (Egyptian hieroglyphs) gives the meaning of Sheti as "to go deeply into a subject; to study profoundly; to search magical books; to penetrate deeply." **Light from Ancient Africa** is a profound study of Sakhu , and while easily read, the reader should go deeply into the* *subject, search for its hidden meaning and penetrate deeply. In effect, we should use this ''light'' to continue our quest for an authentic African psychology or the "**Sakhu Sheti**"--the deep and profound study of the human spirit; or the study, mastery and understanding of the process of human illumination.*

*As you read **Light from Ancient Africa**, think deeply and profoundly and become transformed.*

Wade W. Nobles, Ph.D.
San Francisco State University
June 1994

Table of Contents

INTRODUCTION

The distinguished Senegalese multi-scholar Dr. Cheikh Anta Diop declared that Ancient Egypt was the *classical* civilization of Africa and, in turn, the primal civilization of the world. The prolific British scholar, Gerald Massey, declared that Egypt was the "Light of the World." Certainly these designations of the ancient African land (called "Kemet" by the inhabitants themselves and subsequently called "Egypt" in the inevitable renaming which conquerors impose on their prey) are indicative of the significance of this great and primal world civilization. The unquestionable consensus of all people in all times is that the foundation of all that is claimed as *civilized* in this world has a preliminary presence and manifestation in the Nile Valley development and in contributions on the continent currently called "Africa." Thousands of thinkers and students of Truth have devoted their entire lives to the study of the meaning and contributions of Kemet. Thousands of others, in the pursuit of their separate studies, have had to "cross the Nile" in order to fully appreciate everything from architecture to medicine, religion to astronomy. There is, in fact, no field of study which does not have its foundation in Ancient Kemet.

I am of the latter group. I am not a Kemetologist (Egyptologist). In fact, my knowledge of the history, language and content of this great and mighty civilization is, at best, infantile and, at worst, superficial. I am a great admirer of what I know of this great civilization. I have been tremendously inspired by what I have seen during my several visits to the ruins of this great land and enlightened by what I have understood about the Kemetic understanding of man, God and civilization.

The adage that a little knowledge can be a dangerous thing has frequently proven to be quite true. With a little knowledge, one skates precariously on the thin ice of serious error. One seriously compromises his commitment to truth and accuracy when he tries to scale the mountains of Truth with the short ropes of limited understanding. With this limitation in mind, this small volume is a rendezvous with danger. I cannot enter it without the clear disavowal of several potential misinterpretations and the establishment of a context for the encounter.

My major interest as a student of the mind is to gain an ever-increasing insight into the resources available to human beings in their mental apparatus. This interest is not abstract, but it is very practically and directly tied to the quest for answers to the vast human problems of the historically oppressed, colonized and enslaved human beings of our modern era, namely the people of African descent. My work as a so-called "psychologist" is to gain greater armaments to fight the battle for the liberation of the Black mind. I clearly see the mind of Africa as the primal mind for all humanity and, in identifying the keys for the re-liberation of the mind of Africa, we will free humanity's mind in general. This endeavor is neither a detour nor a diversion from the pursuit of universal Truth. From the insight of the great scholar Dr. W. E. B. DuBois, we recognize that there is no road to the universal except by way of the particular. The particular existential routing that we must choose is that of our social/cultural/historical experience. Despite our frequent critiques of the consequence of having been imposed upon by the experiences of other (conquerors), we do not want to suggest the illegitimacy of their right to seek the universal answers through the affirmation of their particular experience and disposition.

Let me go further in saying what this booklet is not. It is not intended to be a comprehensive analysis of the ancient Kemetic conception of the human mind. It is at best a surface glimpse at some basic and introductory concepts of ways that the ancient Africans understood the human mind. Admittedly we only touch the most rudimentary ideas as both an enticement for others to dig deeper for more information and as an initiation into the depths of understanding possessed by those great and wise Africans of old.

This book is not a complete reflection of the meaning of these ancient African myths and symbols. We accept that the symbolism of Ancient Kemet was like the proverbial onion with layer upon layer of meanings. The power of these ancient African myths is manifested both in their multiple meaning, their adaptability and their longevity. The interpretations that we offer of these ancient stories represent only one layer of interpretation. The validity of these symbols as a methodology for understanding the ideas which we are seeking to identify is only one of their multiple functions. We do not suggest for a minute that this represents all there is to understand about these images.

The purpose of looking back into the vast reservoir of our ancient African ancestors is not at all intended as an invitation to regress or to even dwell in the past. We are, in fact, looking back with the intention of seeing ahead. Despite the greatness of ancient African civilization, it never invites us to go backwards. The entirety of the ancient Kemetic civilization was forward-looking. Our purpose is to use these ancient images as a crystal ball for futuristic perceptions. Our objective is to be visionaries and not seekers after nostalgia. Our objective is to strategize for the future and not to vegetate romantically in the past. Certainly, the images of 4,000 years ago could not have been complete, otherwise the demise of Kemet would not have occurred and the regression of the last 2,000 years would not have occurred. What is clear is that the ancient African minds had reached a significant plateau in human development in this phenomenal Nile Valley civilization. Our efforts are, at least, to understand some of what they had achieved so that we can continue beyond the level of their accomplishment.

The problems of this African American community are tremendous and severe. These problems are not beyond repair, however, if we adopt the correct healing methods to address them. The mental health, social, and educational problems are all solvable if we approach them correctly. Those African American scholars who are suggesting that we look back into our African culture as a foundation for solutions are not suggesting that the answers are there fully-formed for our harvesting. We are suggesting that the foundation for finding solutions will have to be located in a knowledge that existed prior to the exceedingly disruptive experience of our American holocaust. The problems of self-alienation, self-destruction, and the willingness to serve as pawns for the disruption and decay of our communities are not natural problems. We suggest that the overwhelming evidence of African people working against our own progress and effective development cannot be attributed to any constitutional disability on our part. Instead, we consider these highly unnatural problems to be a consequence of the unnatural experiences that we have encountered over the last four centuries. If a people are systematically prevented from engaging in the constructive execution of their life processes and subjected to the dehumanizing experiences of being made servants of an alien culture, then one can predict that they might conceivably act in ways inconsistent with their own development and counter to their best self-interest. It is for this reason that we believe that we must look into the genesis of our natural human experience in order to identify the proper parameters with which to address these issues.

We firmly believe that classical African civilization offers the best glimpse of a meaningful prototype of effective African life. The assumptions about the fundamental ontology which we must adopt, i.e., to see all being as fundamentally spiritual and the ethical standards which must be applied are found in the ruins of what is left of this great civilization. The display of the symbols, the utilization of the myths, or the application of the rituals must be done with great caution and with an eye towards understanding that which permits adaptation. The fundamentalist analysis and application of the principles of this culture only carry us to the same point of confusion that all fundamentalism carries its adherents. We must remain liberal and flexible in our interpretations in order that we extract only the best guidelines for the study and advancement of our modern peoplehood.

The essays in this small volume are all adapted from presentations that I have made in a variety of settings over the last several years. All of those presentations were in one way or another geared towards developing an interpretation of ancient Kemetic thought that would advance the contemporary African American community. In each instance, I was asked to develop a presentation from the vantage point of a psychologist. Therefore, all of these essays are focused from that point of view. The most direct discussion of the relationship of ancient Kemetic thought to modern psychology is found in the lead essay, "Kemetic Origins of Psychology." This essay makes some direct translations of the terminology and concepts of modern psychology as reflected in its origins from the language and concepts of Ancient Kemet.

An effort is made to identify some of the symbols and language from this ancient African culture to understand its conception of the human mind, its processes and its potential. In contrast, we try to identify how modern Western psychology has deviated from its historical teachers and has seriously retarded the human mind's development by its limiting concepts. The ideas in this essay are an excellent example of how the ideas of Ancient Kemet serve not only as a source of directing and correction for the misguided oppressed African people, but to assist all of humanity back to the path of Maat (Truth).

Introduction

The remaining essays use illustrations from Kemetic myths, symbols or metaphysics as a tool to better understand the condition of African people, particularly those enslaved to the Western world. The story of Ausir (called Osiris by the Greeks) is one such symbolic myth. The fundamentalist interpretation of the story of Ausir is to see him as a historical god/man figure who was literally the first king of Kemet. There are those who would go so far as to seek his ancient tomb in an effort to reconstruct his history. Our preferred direction is to think of him as mythological (while understanding that myth is part real and part fantasy; it captures a transcendent and permanent Truth that is more real than fantasy and more surreal than real). This approach lets us use the story of Ausir to gain a real and meaningful understanding of what has happened in our time and recent history. Also implicit in the interpretation are strategies for resolving contemporary problems, which are in part socio-economic, political, cultural, etc., but which are simultaneously spiritual and metaphysical. From this point of view, only myth would suffice because only the myth has portability to move comfortably between these disparate realms of reality.

So we offer this volume of essays in the tradition of the other five books which we have previously written. Our intent is to be readable, affordable, and understandable. I consider myself a lifelong student, and in popular language, probably a scholar. My intention, however, is not necessarily to engage in a scholarly discussion for the stimulation of other scholars. Instead, I want to engage those beginning students and other seekers of truth who may understand neither the scholar's language nor his approach. I must admit that I am somewhat handicapped by my training. I have come to use language and to approach problems in a way that those ''trained'' (not necessarily educated) like myself tend to speak and think. I know that this way of speaking often misses many people who are struggling to grasp these ideas. For this, I apologize. Please understand that I am still trying to communicate in a way that the majority will understand what I am trying to say, rather than just a select minority. If this book is not understandable to people who have the educational level of an eighth grader, then I have failed in my effort. Those with more advanced training may be critical of the book's simplicity, but they will, at least understand it.

Originally, I had planned to call this book *Ancient African Light for Human Transformation*. In addition to this title being somewhat clumsy and rather pretentious, I also thought it might frighten away some readers. Such a high sounding title would certainly attract some few people who want to appear more knowledgeable than they really are, but most folks would keep looking down the shelf for a book that sounded more like real stuff. Actually, ''human transformation'' is still what this book is about. My major objective as an African thinker is to better understand how we can change our form from imperfect to more perfect matter; how we can become ever more excellent; how we can better reach the goal of changing our lives into a form that represents our greatest potential as human beings to be of greater service to ourselves and the rest of humanity. I accept the fact that we enter this life raw and incomplete. We are seeds of great and divinely inspired possibility. The real challenge of life, learning, and growing is to better understand how to reach that goal of more complete growth.

We believe that Ancient Africa has given the world more light on this subject than any other culture. We also believe that the light has been grossly obscured by the intentional distortion of the image of Africa and its people. A part of the task that I see before me and all of us as descendants of the great African contributors to humankind is to restore our ancestors to their former and well-deserved dignity. We can best do this by demonstrating the power of their wisdom through applying it to our lives and our condition. When we show the power of this great light to transform our lives, we will have restored our ancient ancestors to the lofty place of dignity which they so justly deserve. *Light from Ancient Africa* is a contribution to this process. May the Creator and those ancestors be pleased!

I

Kemetic Origins of Psychology[1]

"Egyptology" is not a new pursuit. Since the peak of Kemetic civilization, generations of scholars have devoted themselves to fully understanding the complexities of this pinnacle of human civilization and development. A unique element concerning the contemporary focus on Kemet is its leadership coming from African and African-American scholars, whereas in the past, the course of this exploration was charted by European discretion. Another contemporary factor worth noting is the confirmation that Kemet, at the peak of its development, was fundamentally a Black African society.

The significance of such Kemetic accomplishments transcend race, yet there have been "imposters" who have tried throughout history to exclude the Black presence. The time has come for us to admit and appreciate the obvious: that in Africa, the people are *African*. Therefore, the wisdom of Africa is naturally the wisdom of African people--Black people.

The efforts to rediscover the ancient Kemetic understanding of reality is no less than the "modern" African's quest for redemption. Redemption: restoration, resurrection, the re-establishment of order. Knowledge is the pathway back to this proper order.

Professor George G. M. James (1976) said many years ago that by beginning to assert the source of the higher knowledge of humanity, the universe itself becomes a process of redemption for African people. He says, "This proposition (Greeks were not the authors of Greek philosophy, but the Black people of North Africa, the Egyptians), will become a philosophy of redemption to all Black people when they accept it as a belief and live up to it." (A lot of us accept it as a belief, but few of us are willing to live up to it because of its demanding standards).

Our philosophy for redemption is a psychological process involving a change in behaviors. Professor James said, "It really signifies a mental emancipation in which the Black people will become liberated from the chain of traditional falsehood, which for centuries has incarcerated them in the prison of inferiority complex and world humiliation and insult.'' By understanding and recognizing our imprisonment, we are engaging in a redemptive process.

In order to effectively understand the relevance of the Kemetic concept of the human mind, it is important to understand the rather limited notions of the Western (Judeo-Christian or European) concept of the human being and human functioning. The development of Western Civilization is deficient in many ways. Its technology has far outstripped its appreciation for the specialness of the human being. Western Civilization stifles and pacifies us with vehicles and vessels of technological expression which far exceed our present state of human development.

Western society has basic human problems of greater severity than societies with much less developed technology. Human issues such as love, love-making, parenting and peaceful interaction with other human beings remain fundamental problems for people in the ''Western world.'' Despite all of the technological know-how, the people remain retarded in mastering simple human issues. Such is not the case for many who have never heard of television or cellular phones.

Characteristics of Western Psychology

If we take the meaning of the word ''psychology,'' which the West has distorted and reduced to ''the scientific study of human behavior'', we find the first flaw in Western science. The word ''psyche'' was derived from the Greek language by way of African origin. The word is associated with the goddess Psyche, and to the Greeks meant ''soul.'' According to Massey (1974a) in his *Book of the Beginnings*, the word ''psyche'' is actually derived from the Egyptian language in that ''Khe'' is the soul, and ''Su'' is she: Su-Khe. Su-Khe embodies the nature and meaning of the Greek goddess, Psyche. Without the article ''p'', the Egyptian word ''Sakhu'' means the understanding, the illuminator, the eye and the soul of the being, that which inspires. From this linguistic analysis, we find that not only is the study of the human mind offered to us by the Greeks by way of the Motherland, but the terminology as well.

The distortion of the Kemetic definition changed the study of the _soul_ to the study of _behavior_. Because of this, we find a whole array of consequences which have developed and serve as the basis for many of the problems that we remain plagued with today. Some interesting factors to consider are that:

1. The West views man as an object and emphasizes objective methods for studying him. Their objectivity assumes that all valid knowledge is external, leading one to believe that everything comes from outside (including salvation). This view assumes that the human being is no more than a tabula rasa (blank screen) that is imprinted by things in the environment, and that the only way you can understand man is to objectively stand outside and look at him. Western psychology claims it is not legitimate to ask a man what he thinks. The reasoning for this is because it is considered to be ''unscientific'' and ''unobjective,'' and therefore does not qualify to be legitimate science. ''Objectivity'' is supposedly the virtue of European science, and subjectivity its gravest violation. Introspection and self-awareness, the virtues of ancient Kemetic science, are the ultimate offenses in Western science.

2. Quantification is the only accepted measure of reality in Western science; ''if we can't count it, it's not real.'' According to this logic, there is no such thing as intelligence if you can't put numbers on it. With this school of thought, one could assess that there is no such thing as happiness because it cannot be calculated. With this, one can't even be crazy unless they score accordingly on an ''objective'' measure.

3. The West views material reality as essential. With this logic, the essence of man is assumed to be his material manifestation, i.e. body and behavior. A convenient analogy between the bodies of laboratory rats and that of man is readily drawn, since in this system, the physiological determinants of one are supposedly the same in all related cases. The potential for humans to master and transcend their own physiological aspects has not been clearly addressed in the Western analysis.

4. According to Western thought, there is no superior power or purpose in man. With the hasty dismissal of any superior plan, man's *presence becomes meaningless, an existence with no divine purpose. There can be no expectation of human life if it has no direction or higher meaning.*

5. From the perspective of the West, the observable activities a person engages in is a true picture of his or her essential being: "What you see is what you get." According to Western doctrine, human behavior is what it is with no significant meaning beyond what is actually observed.

6. All invisible or intangible phenomena is considered irrelevant within the Western scientific analysis. It views the soul, spirit, revelation and intuition as superstition or illusions.

7. Life and consciousness are identical with physical processes. This means that the brain is equivalent to the mind. The Western-thinking scientists believe they can understand the functioning of the mind through cosmetic experiments: "If we alter your brain chemically or surgically, the mind , being the passive agent, will naturally become a servant of the chemistry." The chemistry is not ever discussed as the servant of the mind because this would give pre-eminence to the invisible.

8. Western doctrine emphasizes the individuality of the person and generally ignores the element of transpersonal awareness. An "individual" operating under this reasoning is led to believe that there is no meaningful scientific concept such as a group or a collective being. The idea of a collective mind would require an intangible conception of the mental process. It could not be equated with individual brains. The idea that separate physical entities could share a common consciousness borders on the absurd for the typical Western thinker.[2]

9. Western psychology maintains that man is a product of biological determination, personal experiences, and chance. There is no correct or incorrect order for man's development under this reasoning. Once again man finds himself reduced by this logic to an existence like the animals. He inhabits the earth with simply surviving against the odds by adaptation to an environment. With this, morality and values can have no meaning outside of personal experience. Therefore, if there is no order, then you cannot expect people to do anything. People are fundamentally free without the guidelines of a dome (i.e., "free-dome"). Morality and values serve as the frame of the "dome's" structure. Therefore, a Eurocentric thinker assumes that there is no particular purpose, direction or order. Morality becomes meaningless to them. Moral or ordered conduct has no place in their science, except as an extension of one's personal biological ethics. Morality, at best, could only be viewed as a temporary environmental adaptation.

10. A characteristic of the Western science of the mind is the opinion that the death of the body is the death of the mind, and that one need not attend to life before or after the body (i.e. "You only live once, man"). This limited concept imprisons the human being into a linear existence which begins at birth and ends at physical death. Human beings as timeless creatures have yet to be recognized or understood by Western science.

The idea of ultimate transformation is a meaningless concept in this time and space-limited designation of human life. Such narrow conceptions of the human being inevitably lead to narrow conceptions of the mind and its potential. Non-Western concepts of mental mastery, transcendence and mental or spiritual pre-eminence are empty and reek of superstition and ignorance. Simply put, Western psychology can conceive only limited and small beings, confined by physical matter, time and space.

The Psychology of Ancient Kemet

The wisdom of Ancient Kemet is like a vast tapestry of amazing complexity, with colors and dimensionality, covering the full range of man's collective potential. Each thread of the tapestry has been carefully woven such that every thread is defined by every other. It remains intact only because every thread is present. No thread can be unraveled without destroying the tapestry.

Such is the task facing anyone who dares to explore any thread of the knowledge of Ancient Kemet. The bountiful preservation and excavations supply the Egyptologists with abundant material for the study of the life, beliefs, and theology of Ancient Kemet. An encyclopedic volume of work is available to researchers from any component of the Kemetic existence. And yet the true science of Ancient Kemet still remains essentially unknown.

Because of the complexity of the Kemetic worldview, it is very difficult to concentrate exclusively on certain components of this sophisticated system of thought. In the Kemetic realm, one cannot make distinctions between psychology, physics, chemistry, mathematics, art, religion and philosophy. Such divisions are meaningless in the Kemetic conception of a universe where everything was related to everything else. Such wholistic understanding is completely counter to the analytical fragmentation which characterizes the Western approach to understanding.

There is no such distinction as sacred versus secular; there is no such thing as the life of this world and the life of the other world, no such thing as the religious versus the political. Everything is tied intimately and inextricably together. To enter a fragmented discussion such as identifying a category of study that is "psychology" is a fundamental discredit to Kemetic intelligence. This "modern artificial approach" to comprehension plagues the contemporary understanding of the *spherical reality* of Ancient Kemet. It forces the range of Kemetic thought into the square or linear analysis of the West.

Even though psychology as a segregated entity does not exist in the studies of the ancient Kemetic realm, it is important to remember that it views man as the fundamental metaphor for all higher truth--the antennae through which all information and intelligence in the universe can pass. The understanding of man was viewed as paramount in the science of Ancient Kemet.

The ingenious study of religion, science, mathematics, psychology, and government is the study of man and his potential. It is significant to note that Western scientists write off subjects such as astrology, alchemy, and numerology as being superstition. The scientists of Ancient Kemet understood that you could not talk about mathematics without talking about the human being.

Ancient Kemetic numerology talks about the relationship between symbolic quantification and human expression. This African civilization's study of alchemy addresses the connection between the transformation of materials in nature with the transformative potential in the human psyche. So alchemy is actually meta-chemistry, not superstitious chemistry. It is not less than, but greater than. Of course when the materialistic Europeans sought to apply such wholistic principles of metascience, they wanted only to make material gold out of material lead, rather than golden character from the raw lead of undeveloped human expression. Such reductionism distorts the true essence of being. Ancient Kemetic science was both actual and metaphorical, empirical and invisible.

The African study of the stars (astrology) examines the relationship between the human process and the celestial process, recognizing a connection between the two and their inseparability. They realized that human development aligns itself, and is related to, the celestial order and process. Therefore, the evolution of mind is akin to the evolution of the heavens. The movement, timing, and consistency of nature is integral to understanding the development of the mind. So alchemy, astrology and numerology must all be rediscovered--in their original form. Man is a microcosm, and in understanding man, one understands the macrocosm that is all of nature (the universe).

Consciousness or awareness is the ultimate goal in the Kemetic concept of the mind. The dictum, ''man know thyself'', is the fundamental principle of the psychology of Kemet. George G. M. James (1976) observed that the doctrine of self-knowledge was for centuries attributed to the Greek, Socrates. It is now definitely known to have originated from Egyptian temples. On the outside of such temples, the words ''man know thyself'' were written and still can be seen today.

During the zenith of the Kemetic society, one could not enter into the instruction of the temples until the fundamental principle of development was understood. The foundation of consciousness, growth and psychological development are rooted in this principle. Professor James goes on to say that ''self-knowledge, then, is the basis of all true knowledge.'' The mastery of passions was required as the first step, the taming of the wild inner beast, putting the inner beast under the control of the higher being.

Passions run wild in the psyche when left untamed. When passions are allowed to rule, there is no opportunity for the higher powers to gain control. The passionate lower nature, therefore, must be rendered dormant in order to permit the higher powers to reign. This is the meaning of the very popular image of the Sphinx in the Kemetic symbolism. The Sphinx illustrates the subdued lower nature in the form of a wild lion tamed under the ruling head (mind) of the fully developed human consciousness.

The second step required the neophyte to become acquainted with the higher powers in themselves. One must come to know the divine form which inhabits his/her being. This is the function of education into the "mysteries." Each human being must know the confrontation of Ausir and Set that acts within himself. The labors of Auset and the ultimate victory of Heru are part of the life process. The study of the "mysteries" was a study of the forces and the mastery of those forces in one's own being.

"Man know thyself" was more than a theoretical posture. It was an invitation to view one's mind as the stage on which this divine drama repeats itself again and again. One's ultimate responsibility as the theatrical director of this drama is necessary for the successful development of their own psyche.

The basis of the word "education" comes from Ancient Kemet and is based on the understanding that all one needs to know is inside the self. This African civilization viewed education as the structuring of an environment to educe (bring out) the higher potential of that person. The "logos" (meaning) of the "psyche" (soul) is the concept the Greeks were taught by their teachers in Kemet. This is how the Greeks received their "psychology." The African teachers instructed the Greeks to view the objective of psychology as the objective of life: *to gain awareness of the full dimensionality of the soul.*

There is good reason to believe that Kemetic architectural and political structures stood as illustrations of this higher awareness. For example, the royal crowns of Upper and Lower Kemet reflect the principle of complimentarity in human consciousness. The pharaoh's wearing of this double crown speaks of Kemet's political unification in itself.[3] This crown also reflects the unification of consciousness. It probably offered the first suggestion to understanding the dual hemispheres of the brain (which have only recently been rediscovered in Western science). A physical image of higher truth itself is illustrated in the analogy of the varying functions and emphasis of Ancient Upper and Lower Kemet. Its pyramids and technically advanced structures epitomize the rational sphere found predominantly in Lower Kemet. When the components operate together wholistically, there is no clear distinction between these spheres. The dwelling place of the Divinites was relegated to Upper Kemet, the spiritual (or wholistic) sphere. It was only when Kemet was unified that the greatest advancements were made. This union synthesizes the ostensible duality of consciousness and made it (as well as the mind) one.

The presence of the serpent (or Uraeus) on the front of the double crown of the King symbolizes the upright readiness of the soul (housed in one's pineal gland).[4] The synthesized Uraeus, stands as a symbol of the enlightened soul.

The Dimensions of the Soul

The tombs of Ancient Kemet are vivid testimonials to their profession of faith in the ultimate survival of the soul. As we understand the dimensions of the soul, we are introduced to the vastness of the human potential. What follows is a very brief and purposely oversimplified introduction to the Kemetic dimensions of the person.[5]

The first dimension of the soul is called the **Ka**. The whole notion of Ka is viewed as being the body of the person--one's physicality. In other words, the Ka is the stabilizing principle that contains and synthesizes one's spiritual energy. The Ka is the earthly appearance of man. Life, therefore, inhabits what is known as the Ka. The Ka becomes more defined with several levels. There is a divine Ka, which is viewed as the original Ka of the Creator, which is the source of man's body as a human being. There is the intermediate Ka, which consists of nature's minerals, vegetables, animal life, etc. The intermediate Ka deals with how these aspects of nature operate and the forms they take on as a manifestation of spiritual energy (these are also the constituents and the nourishments of the human form).

There is the inferior Ka. It is one's personal body, or Ka. It speaks to those inherited characteristics which are unique from person to person. The objective of the person, or the goal of the person's inner development, is to be able to bring the inferior Ka up to divine Ka. Therefore, the cultivation of one's character represents the ongoing transformation from the inferior, individualized, separate, isolated physical self to a more transcendent self. We find this state of being as the highest human form--the Divine body. This picture again shows man as the "microcosm." He integrates in his being the entire cosmos.

When going deeper into the aspect of the human make-up, we find the <u>Ba</u>. The Ba is the breath of the soul, entering into and activating the being of a person. Rather than identifying this element as some anthromorphic God breathing into the man (Adam), these ancient Africans symbolized this as the living form of a bird with a human head. This earthly and celestial bird combines with the person's (inferior) Ka and spirit to generate a living being. The picture language of the ancient wise ones gave living illustrations of higher truths.

This soul of breath represents the transmission of invisible energy source (like electricity), running through the visible and living entities. Ancient Kemet states that there is only one power, which is symbolically represented as the breath. This power of breath is transmitted from the ancestors to the descendants, all the way back to the Creator.[6] This cycle illustrates the belief that this power or energy will always exist. The <u>Ba</u> is, in effect, the vital principle which represents the essence of all things.

The Ba and the Ka both operate as complements to each other. The activating life (Ba) and the passive physical form of the Ka unite to form a cooperative relationship that exists until death on this plane. At the time of mortal death, the Ka remains to be restored to the earth as Ba returns to the heavens. Ba takes with it the divine part of Ka--back to its originator.

The <u>Khaba</u> is the shade or covering soul corresponding to the notion of the ghost. It is the astral or etheric body. It is related to the so-called Akashic records,[7] which holds the memories of all the pictures or imaginings from our collective evolution.

It is the Khaba (called Khabit by some) which produces emotion and motion. It is also thought to be responsible for sustaining the sensory perceptions, the phenomena of color, harmony, or rhythm, and the circulation of blood. So the drums and the rituals in many West African societies were used as a means of stimulating the Khaba, because in stimulating the Khaba, one was re-immersed into the Akashic records. It is important to note the worldwide influence of Ancient Kemet--even in linguistics. Khaba, being Ancient Kemet's culmination of both Ka and Ba, also became the name of the sacred synthesizing spot of pilgrimage for the Muslims of Mecca (commonly referred to as the "Black Stone"). It is at the Khaba where all humanity comes together and becomes one in a Divine transformation of unity.

The African descendants in Haiti and South America induce spiritual state or trance by beating rhythms which stimulate the Khaba. What the West calls "spirit possession" is actually the expression of the Khaba. The person is not so much possessed as they are in an elevated state of consciousness. This consciousness permits the Khaba to express itself from the ancient (Akashic) records.

Westerners, in a sense, conceive of the mind as the seat of our rational functions. This is obviously related to the **Akhu**. The Akhu is the fourth dimension of the psychic nature. It is described as the seat of intelligence and mental perception. It is in the arena of the Akhu, the Ancients believed, that the whole mystery of the human mind is to be comprehended.

The Ancient Africans considered the Akhu to be the navigator of the human spirit, but only during physical life. The concern of the mind was primarily the survival of its own thinking process. The Akhu is characterized by attributes like judgement, analysis and mental reflection, all of which can be channeled so as to be dedicated to the higher being. In other words, the Akhu never was intended to be rational in and of itself. It never makes judgements and analyses based upon its own perspective.

Intelligence, therefore, is intended to be nothing more than a servant to the higher being, or Divine Ka. In the ancient Kemetic realm, intelligence was considered to be located in the heart. It is not only considered to be rational, but also spiritual and ethical. Akhu perceives the principles of Maat.[8] It permits a fusion between reason and attributes such as harmony, truth, compassion, justice, etc.

In Ancient Kemet, the test of intelligence would unfold at the judgement of the deceased. When Anubis guides the deceased into the court of Ausir (judge of the Divine Ka), the deceased one's heart (Akhu) is place on the scale of justice. One's intelligence is measured by whether or not the heart has been so lightened that it will not tilt a feather on the other side of the scale. The feather symbolizes "Maat." The imagery finds expression in the *Holy Qur'an*, which says, "We shall set up scales of justice for the day of Judgement, so that not a soul will be dealt with unjustly in the least'' (XXI:47).

If the test is passed, it means that one has used their intelligence to cultivate harmony in their ethical or moral being. One can achieve this feat by having used their intelligence to transform a corrupt society to a purified one. Further cultivating the world (as opposed to destroying it) is the key to passing this crucial test. One should use their intelligence, not to feed passion, but to elevate and transcend it so that the heart becomes (en)lightened. Only at this level will passion be relieved of its earthly weight and the gravity that ties it to the inferior Ka, which restricts its ascendance to the Divine.

The **Seb** is the soul of pubescence. Seb does not manifest in humans until puberty or adolescence. The evidence of Seb's presence is the power of the human being to generate its own kind. The Seb is, in effect, the self-creative power of being. This is the element that Freud extracted from Kemetic logic and used to formulate his theory which suggested: ''This is all that we are.'' Freud's ''sex'' took the ''b'' out and made it ''x'', changing seb to sex. We are created, but we have been given the capability to also reproduce ourselves. Creativity is the principle contained in the reproductive capacity. This is the real meaning of ''libido'' or life-force that Freud reduced to ''pleasure-seeking energy.''

The **Putah** is the intellectual soul of the first intellectual father. Unlike the Akhu, the Putah was associated with the mental maturity of the individual--the union of the brain with the mind. This is the establishment of the human identity. With the attainment of Putah, the will and intent alone came to govern conduct. The maturity of the Putah represents the person's ability to reproduce *intellectually*--the ability to teach others.

The Putah recognizes that self-discipline and identity as understood through purpose are the necessary prerequisites for becoming a teacher. African people naturally revere the wisdom of the elders because elders reflect the maturity of intelligence. The Putah is a component of the self, but is an attainment that evolves with the growth and transformation of the self.

Finally, we come to the **Atum**. This is the seventh division of the psyche and is considered the divine or eternal soul. In some text, it is identified with the seventh creation. The deity Atum inspires the breath of life everlasting. In ritual, this division represents itself as parenthood, the symbol of full creative powers and perpetual continuation.

Some writers talk about a synthesis or an integration of these seven divisions of the psyche into an eighth. Others speak of the seventh as being an integration itself. Those who talk about the eighth as a separate division (such as Massey, 1974b) speak of this higher synthesis as being the Heru or the Christ of the personality. (This not Jesus the man, but the Christ consciousness attained by the man Jesus. It represents a capacity for all people as they approach the Divine Ka and achieve personal integration).

The integration, or synthesis, of all the components of the personality represents the emergence of Heru, or the Christ, in the human form. This component is described as the ultimate destiny of the soul, the Ka of God.

II

FINDING THE AFRICAN SELF

Who are you? What is the "self"? Most people you ask will have a different answer. Some people define themselves by their sex. Some will tell you what they do, or where they live, or how many degrees they have. Others will trot out their religious or social affiliations, or their political beliefs.

The muddiness of the definition of "self" has caused conflict through the ages, a conflict that is especially destructive to the modern African American community. We simply do not have the luxury to get caught up in the confusion that emanates from the wrong formulation of the self that is based on illusion and superficiality.

Our African ancestors had it right. These ancient Kemetic people were humanity's elders - not just our elders. They fathered much of the human knowledge that is known or that is to be known. They tell us that the only way to understand anything and the only knowledge that is substantial knowledge is that which answers the greatest question of all: *"What is the nature and the progression of the soul?"* Our Nile Valley elders committed their entire culture/science to understanding the problem of mapping the journey of the soul. Their development of the Sphinx, the Pyramid, mythology, symbols, songs, drama, art, and the sciences all pointed toward this end. Their concept of the "soul" became fundamental to understanding the "self."

We want to suggest to you a way to understand the nature of the confusion with regard to the definition of self, and draw upon classical African knowledge as a means of trying to grasp the definitions that our ancestors put forward. This discussion is intended to be more than theory. Our goal is that it will also serve as a roadmap to move us as a people forward and to make positive changes in ourselves and in our communities.

Ka: The Soul of Blood

Are we the same, or are we all different? The Ancients approached this question in a way that is completely different from those who deal in Western science. The latter have botanists, biologists, and zoologists who categorize people, plants, and animals, according to superficial differences commonly know as "genus" or "species." In Western thought, there is a tremendous preoccupation with differentiating the various aspects of nature. If a butterfly has a wing shape that is round as opposed to having a peak, it is one kind of butterfly. If a particular beaver has one kind of color on the end of its tail, it is one genus as opposed to another genus.

Western psychology does the same thing. It is involved in the Western scientific definitional process, and once again emphasizes "difference." Western psychologists are concerned with how each of us *differs* from the other.

The Ancients, on the other hand, looked at the "essence of sameness." They taught that things and people should be defined, not by their appearance, but by their essence. They understood and appreciated distinction and differentiation, but they never made distinction an end in itself. Instead, it was always used as an instrument to understand the commonality and uniformity. They saw *unity* as the essential message around which all things operated. The definition of the self was only superficially described by observable characteristics and qualities. The real story had to do with the *self*, a word which, in their language, was equivalent to the *soul*.

What does this have to do with the blood? Plenty. The blood that courses through your body and keeps you alive is, itself, the essence of physical life. That blood is not just "your" blood; it is the blood that came from your mother, which came to her from her mother, and so on. Remember that nine months before you came into this world, the blood that you have was interchangeable with your mother's. The Ancients called this blood, that passed down through the ages, "Ka."

There is an important lesson in this observation. It tells us that "individuality" is an illusion. Our blood that we receive at birth is not even our blood. It tells us that we have nothing to protect except what has been given to us. The blood that flows through our veins was loaned to us. It was transmitted by ancestors who did the job of surviving.

Those things which previous generations have already endured, confronted, and overcome are passed on in the blood. There are many diseases and other environmental battles that we do not have to fight because the blood of our ancestors has conquered those enemies and passed the trophies down to us. From them we have inherited not only physical characteristics, but also a structural consciousness of accumulated wisdom and "light." We are thoroughly connected with each other as a family.

Your body is not your own. It was loaned to you to move you through this life. The body is a tool and a dwelling place that provides us with a high precision instrument to operate within the physical world. It is the physical world's contribution to our whole make-up in this world.

Ba: The Essence of Self

What the Ancients call "Ba" is what we traditionally think of as the soul. It is that which stays with you even when you leave the physical body. The ancient Egyptian (Kemetic) writers portrayed the Ba as a bird with a human head, signifying that the soul has "wings" which leave the body after death. *(See Fig. 1)*

The Ancients saw the Ba as the *essence* of the self. This concept--that the soul is your essence--is repeated in the Scriptures, but many who hold to Judeo-Christian and Islamic thought see the soul as just a part of the human makeup rather than its very core. Understanding the difference is critical to those who want to move toward a unified concept of the self.

The Ba is actually the natural soul. It represents a combination of spirit and intelligence. It is the energy that comes directly from the Creator, and it is our continued link to the Creator. The Ba, unlike the Ka, which has been transformed through the experiences of our ancestors, is the original creative energy of the Creator. It is the Ba which is the so-called "Breath of Life" that is talked about in the Book of Genesis.

"Breath" is an allegory for the universality of the life force that runs through all of us. Breath and life come from the air. Even the carbon dioxide that plants breathe comes from the air. No one has an exclusive

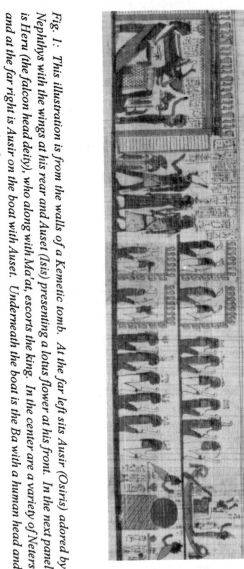

Fig. 1: This illustration is from the walls of a Kemetic tomb. At the far left sits Ausir (Osiris) adored by Nephthys with the wings at his rear and Auset (Isis) presenting a lotus flower at his front. In the next panel is Heru (the falcon head deity), who along with Ma'at, escorts the king. In the center are a variety of Neters and at the far right is Ausir on the boat with Auset. Underneath the boat is the Ba with a human head and arms on the body of a bird.

right over air.

What does this mean? It means that we were created in God's image. Are you looking for the Creator's face? You will find it in the image of the Ba, which is a part of your makeup. Your awareness of its presence gives you access to its resources.

Caucasians have historically tried to re-make God in their image. That is racist and idolatrous. God is not on a wall somewhere, at least in the physical sense. He does not look like you or me, and He certainly is not a Caucasian male with blue eyes. Bowing down to images of God as a white man is spiritual assassination! It is one of the worst things you can do to the souls of Black people, and one of the most insidious forces keeping us in psychological slavery.[9]

Ab: The Soul's Heart

Our Egyptian (Kemetic) ancestors enjoyed and found meaning in word plays. The Ab (same as Akhu in previous chapter), in their thought, becomes a mirror reflection, both in definition and in spelling of the Ba. Whereas the Ba is a spiritual presence or concept, the Ab is its physical manifestation, if you will, the "heart" of the self.

This heart is not the physical heart. It is the symbolic image of the way that people process and merge rational and ethical thinking. The Book of Proverbs tells us to "guard your heart, for out of it flows the issues of life" (Proverbs 4:23). The *Holy Qur'an* says, "This is it (the Qur'an) revealed, that we may strengthen the heart thereby..." (XXV:32).

Rational and ethical thinking can be vastly different. Let's first take a look at ethics.

What is ethics? Is it a listing of "thou shalt nots"? No, it represents an intuitive understanding of the natural order. *Everyone* who is born into the world has an understanding of what it is to be in accord with certain principles of life.

Remember when your elders used to say to you, "You know better than that?" How did you "know" better? Had someone given you a list of the behaviors that were appropriate and inappropriate? No. They assumed that you knew, intuitively, that a certain behavior was not befitting you as a human being.

Does that mean there is no room for instruction? Certainly not. We as parents or elders or guardians must take the responsibility to instruct all of our children. What this does mean is that we are given a certain amount of "light" when we come into the world.

The African way of thinking about this issue is instructive. Western society, in many aspects, has more problems with its members "doing wrong" than do other societies. Here is the problem: Western societies do not believe in morality as a part of the essence of the human makeup. They view conscience as an imposition on the "natural" animal makeup of the human being.

But it is impossible to turn away from the light and not be affected. We did not realize that people who reject natural morality develop a "hard-hearted" mentality. One factor that has fueled racist conduct is the loss of the natural conscience among Western people in this area.

No one told us that our oppressors' hearts were hard. We refused to recognize the indicators. A hard-hearted person will not respond to appeals of morality or human decency. A hard-hearted person will only become harder and angrier under the righteously outraged gazes of those who confront their wrong-doing. Hard-hearted people only redouble their efforts to oppress and attack.

Our history as former slaves provides quite a contrasting picture. We came off the plantation after a three-hundred year- long holocaust that cost us tens of millions of Black lives. We were castrated, killed, destroyed, trampled on, and treated like dogs. Yet we were the first to say, "We forgive you. Let's work together and let bygones be bygones. Just give us our forty acres and a mule and we will be happy."

During the 1960's Civil Rights Movement, we dealt in good faith with some of the most insane, hard-hearted bigots in the world. We bowed in submission when they came out with their wild dogs, their night sticks, and even their guns. We thought we could generate a human response of moral indignation from the attacker with our non-violent tactics.

Such non-violent tactics only seem to work when you are dealing with people who have a functioning conscience. When those consciences have been seared through years of ignoring and neglecting the light, the best response is to wipe the dust off of your feet and separate to build a world apart from their irrational and unethical rantings and ravings. Integration has largely failed us as a people because of our failure to build from our own ethical bases.

Where are our institutions? Where are our movies? Where are our books? Where are our symbols and our heroes? The answers to those questions are our responsibility, which must grow out of conviction based upon our understanding of who and what we are.

We can actually be weighed down in our hearts by ignoring our conscience. Your heart can get "lighter," to the extent that it grows in knowledge, reason and faithful response to the light.

The heart also becomes "heavy" when ritualized behavior becomes your way of responding to the light. Often, blind followers of ritual have the most immoral inner and hidden lives. That is hypocrisy. It happened in the days of the Pharisees and Sadducees. It happened when Europeans used Christianity and Arabs used Islam to justify slavery. It is, unfortunately, happening now with many of the televangelists. There must be a consciousness of "right" from the light or it dims into hypocrisy and evil.

True morality combines reason with an intuitive sense of right and respect--for the Creator, for yourself, and for nature.

The Khabit: Motion and Emotion

The Khabit is the aspect of the self that the ancestors tell us relates to the emotions and the sensory processes, or motion. The two thoughts are parallel. Motion has to do with outer processes, while emotion has to do with inner processes. The Khabit is the way you see, hear, and integrate, or perceive things. Some writers call this the "shadow." Oriental writers called it the astral or ethereal body.

Emotions enable you to have a "body" outside of a body. They help you to give expression beyond yourself. Some especially sensitive people can read these inner movements just by looking at a person. That is where the expression "vibes" comes from. Certain emotions create a system of vibrations from people that can actually be sensed without words. It is also related to the concept of "auras"--the varying "colors" of light that you give off according to your emotional state.

So, contrary to the philosophies of Europeans such as Freud and Skinner, we are more than a set of instinctual animals or programmed responses that can only be changed by "behavior modification" or some other shallow technique. We have vast human potential and are energy "generators" rather than simply "reactors." Our creation is in the form of the Creator and has the same capacity for creativity. We ultimately have responsibility for these Divine qualities which we have been given.

The Seb: Procreation is More Than Just "Having Babies"

The Seb is another aspect of the self. This represents the procreational soul. It is the physical form related to the physical ability for procreation. Our ancestors believed that the Seb came into the person at the time of puberty. It is an expansion of the self, since it brings in another kind of expression and capability.

We procreate in many ways. We talked about the process of procreating via the blood of the mother, and we have talked about intellectual procreation, which is done by building of knowledge and symbols that are transmitted to subsequent generations. The Seb brings in yet another aspect having to do with the ability to procreate new life.

The Ancient Africans in the Nile Valley understood procreations as a spiritual responsibility despite the physicality involved in the process. This is why they instituted highly significant "rites of passage" for boys and girls who entered the adolescent time period. Circumcision, introduced by the people of Ancient Kemet, was performed at this time to instruct the youth of the responsible use of their procreative capacity. The removal of the foreskin represented the death of the boy and birth of the man. The process, if you think about it, replicates symbolically the emergence of the head of the infant from the mother's womb.

These rites of passage taught certain principles. First, the ability to procreate life is more than just "making babies." When you procreate, you must be willing to help "create" the mental/spiritual life that is contained in the physical being you helped produce. You must be willing to spend time and energy as part of the creative process.

We as African Americans have excessively "multiplied" instead of "procreated" because of our unwillingness to understand our responsibilities to the children--our own as well as others. This disorder, emerging from slavery, eliminated the ritualized and rational procedures for guiding the Seb. In order to restore the power of the Seb, we must rebuild the rituals and teachings that restore true procreation. To build a mind that unifies the rational aspect and the spiritual aspect is an act of procreation. That brings us to the last aspect of the self: the Sakhu.

The Sakhu: Synergy of Mind and Spirit

The Sakhu represents the synthesizing capability of the self. It recognizes that you are capable of rational as well as spiritual thought and perception. It is actually a part of the maturing process by which you unify the rational and spiritual processes to become a real homo-sapien or "thinking being." This "melding" creates synergy in the way that you are able to respond to life circumstances.

In fact, synthesis is a recurring theme in all of the components of the self. The main point is that these separate, yet in many ways similar, definitions are all aspects of a whole. They cannot be understood separately.

The Sphinx is itself an ancient image that displays the synthesized processes of the self. The androgynous head is indicative of both masculine and feminine qualities and it symbolizes the intellectual or rational and the capacity for self-mastery. The animal body represents humankind's powerful physical capabilities tamed and transformed by a "balanced" head.

Sakhu is the ancient Egyptian (Kemetic) root of the Greek word "psyche."[10] The psyche came to represent the composite of the entire self. In Sakhu, the Greeks apparently adopted a synthesized abbreviation of the self's processes. These processes were more fully elaborated in the full Kemetic system which we have described above. "Psychology" became the way of describing the synergy which represented the whole self working as a unit.

Sakhu identifies the self as a unit. Despite components of independent function, the self is more than "just the sum of its parts." An illustration of this idea is how the tree is more than root, bark, leaves, and fruit, but an entity that combines those components while recognizing their independent function. Sakhu represents the synergized entity resulting from the combination of Ka, Ba, Khabit, Ab, and Seb.[11]

A Call to Action

Let's begin putting the various aspects of the self back together to make a whole concept. We can continue with our illustration of the tree from the previous section. The root system, or life force, is the Ba, connecting past, present and future. There are also bark, limbs, and leaves: the Seb, Khabit and Sakhu. Those are the *expressions* of you, but not your *essence*. The fact that you play music well is an expression of you, but it is not you. Your ability to be a good parent is an expression of you, but it is not you. It is simply a manifestation of what comes off the tree.

The tree is also a good description of the collective makeup. Our collective rootedness has its beginnings in original African philosophies, philosophies upon which many of the major religions built their principles. Our African ancestors articulated it, developed it, and then actually lost sight of it: This rootedness must be restored.

As long as you understand your connection to the tree and that your fruit, flower, bark, or wood is something of value to the life of the tree, then you are valuable. It does not matter where you came from. That is the key picture we must begin to understand. We should expect different manifestations, but understand the same essence--that which is the collective consciousness of the principles and aspects of the African self.

No one religion or group has a monopoly on the Truth. We can learn from anyone who has responded to the light they have been given. We can claim that which is true and discard that which battles with the light.

It is good to know these things. It is good to understand who you are and what you are made of. But also remember that this knowledge has direct implications for action.

Answering the Call

Knowledge is not something you just collect or store. If it does not stir you to activity, then it is nothing but wasted activity. It is useless, meaningless, and non-productive. It may feel good, but it does nothing. If you go to Egypt and do not come back compelled to change Paris, or Switzerland, or Cleveland, then your study is useless. If the ideas of the Ancients do not impel you to redefine your area of control, your sphere of influence, you do not really understand what you think you understand. At the very least, the knowledge should spur you to say, "I know who I am now. I cannot be a fool. I must take control of my life and insure the advancement of that life.

Knowledge should give us the inspiration to want to make our mark on the world. Any person who knows his/her greatness should want to do something to manifest who they are. The power to transform our condition comes from this knowledge of who we are.

Consider the Scarab

The Ancient Africans could take the most humble picture and draw from it the most profound ideas. One of the most beautiful of these is that of a Scarab.

The little Scarab (dung beetle) is probably one of the most humble creatures on earth. You can observe in its journey an allegory for the journey of the soul.

First of all, Scarabs are born in the water, as we are. Water represents the universal life force, universal regeneration. The earth is mostly water. Our very bodies are largely water. Without water, life is impossible. The *Holy Qur'an* says, "We made from water every living thing"(XXI:30).

What is water? Water is the purifying force. It is a spiritual force. Christian imagery around the "new birth" speaks of water. Water is a powerful image that purifies, cleanses, and transforms physically, mentally, and spiritually. It cools the flame of the fire. It stills the wind. It regulates excess. It is a leveling, synthesizing, mediating device.

Secondly, the Scarab is androgynous, i.e., male and female in one body. Now I am certainly not suggesting, by any means, a "unisex" society. I am suggesting that the Western focus is so excessively on difference and separation, that it has distorted the concept of masculinity and femininity such that the two are viewed in direct opposition to each other. The Western world emphasizes traditional role differences between men and women, some of which come, not from true understanding, but from a distorted traditional "ideal."

Our focus must be different. We must understand the "complementary responsibility" we have, as male and female, to each other. How can my maleness make you a better female? How can your femaleness make me a better male? How can we begin to understand and accept each other, and in the process, better understand ourselves?

We, then, must learn to differentiate only for the purpose of unifying. We must learn to differentiate to understand the nature of the whole. We understand who we are by coming together with the opposite of who we are. We can then move to think in terms of the inner soul, which transcends sexual differentiation. In other words, the part of you which extends beyond death is neither male nor female.

Life is always a cooperative process. It is a process that brings together the energies of male and female. You need both to build a society and a culture. You cannot oppress one and exalt the other. We cannot have great men without great women and vice versa. We must be committed and responsible to one another. A unisexual culture - that is one separate from the opposite sex - will never fully build the self of which we have been speaking.

Take that one step further. There are those who think that the physical coupling of man and woman is the primary way that males and females should come together. They are sadly mistaken. It is possible to have a sexual relationship and not be a part of the relationship. True interaction is holistic and must occur at multiple levels, exploring the full range of human contact. That means that, just as men and women need to understand and interact with one another, men also need to interact with other men and women with other women, to reflect on who they are. The nature of this interaction, of course, differs from the male/female form, but it requires us to know ourselves through others like ourselves.

Let us stop worrying about how men or women should look, or how they should conduct themselves. Instead, let us be cognizant of the fact that male/female struggles are images of the struggle between the known and unknown parts of ourselves. The fusion of these opposites in the androgynous Scarab gave the Ancient Africans a picture of our transcendent destiny.

Thirdly, the Scarab procreates in a most interesting way. It takes balls of dung and rolls from east to west with its hind legs while facing the sun. It is oriented by the light, yet moves backwards from the source of the light. The Scarab follows the movement of the sun.

This parallels the movement of the human soul. The Ancients, through studying the Scarab, saw the importance of the soul being oriented to the light. Growth results from movement in the earth (work) while being oriented by the sun (knowledge and truth).

Let's reflect further about this procreation process. We mentioned that the Scarab moves the dung ball with its hind legs. It then places eggs in the dung and allows the dung to house, or be a ''womb'' to, these budding new lives.

If you study this animal, you will find that it follows some definite rules. The dung ball is a perfect sphere, every time. It is buried in the earth for precisely 28 days--never a day early, never a day late. This tells us that there are laws, that there are correct ways of doing things. Nature obeys strict order, order that we do not always understand. Understanding that order is part of the work of the scientist. Even the instinctual process is mathematically precise. Orderly life is mathematics.

We can take the analogy of the dung ball one step further. The growth of the soul is not something that is earned from the apparent riches of the material world. If the prenatal Scarab can prepare for life in a womb made of dung, certainly we should be able to see the potential for growth and development in any circumstance. The *Holy Qur'an* states that milk which nourishes life comes from between the blood and the feces.

Perhaps the emphasis on trying to simply alter the conditions of ''poverty'' is a wrong emphasis. Perhaps we should concentrate on altering the perceptions and experiences of people about who they really are. If we alter their perceptions, they can begin to alter their conditions.

To live in poverty is definitely not a desirable condition, but an enlightened life in poverty is better than a wealthy life in darkness.

Who knows? Maybe we African Americans are spiritual "Scarabs." Maybe we were dropped here on this ball of dung called North America to help develop our human consciousness to a higher level of evolution, in the excrement of slavery, brutality, and racism. Maybe for a mathematically precise period, our regenerated soul has been waiting to be born.

I want to take one more liberty here - there is so much we can learn from the Scarab! The work of rolling that ball of dung into a perfect sphere, burying it into the ground, and then putting it into the water after exactly 28 days is precisely that - work. We do not have the luxury as African Americans to engage in esoteric thought that avoids the concept of hard work. Stop romanticizing African thought and philosophy and do something! Get some money and build a school. Open up a business. Build stores that sell merchandise that we need. Design fashions that will make us look good. Solve a global problem - or at least work on it. Go somewhere and dig in the earth. Get us some ore. Get us some gold. Get us some iron. Let's build houses, factories, museums, institutions. Let's make the earth different. Let's work at producing new life with the dedication of the Scarab.

We do not have to go to Ghana to do it. Let's do it in Harlem. Let's do it in Mississippi. Let's change it here. That is what it means to put the seeds into the dung ball in the earth. We have to stop only talking - something we are especially good at - and start doing. We have to use our energy, our efforts, and our intellect to transform the structure of the society and to transform ourselves. This is real power!

The journey of the soul (or "Ba") has gone from its conception at the source of life (which is the "idea" that came from the "word" sent into the earth) to roll through the difficulties of the earth, ending up in the water to be reborn. It is transformed and becomes ready to make the world a new place. We are all scarabs. But, according to this ancient symbol, we are also products of the Scarab who was a symbol of Ra (or God). So the model for our human form is the Creator of the universe who is both the Mother and Father of all.

III

RAMESES AND THE DIVINE KINGSHIP: A SPIRITUAL LEGACY

We, as people of African descent living in America, must struggle to thrive in a world that works quite differently from the African world which gave us birth. Africans, like other peoples around the world, live and work within a defined philosophical context and operate according to certain rules and principles. Their perspectives on time, space, God, man, and nature were and are very different from the European perspective.

Americans of all races (and we must include people of African descent here because we live and must work within the confines of a culture that is dominantly European) have a distorted, confused view of African reality and philosophy. Those who endeavor to study and interpret ancient African thought must first understand the way that Africans defined key aspects of life. When we try to interpret the African way of life by superimposing our own definitions and perspectives on that way, we are destined to severely distort our understanding of African thought.

One of the most important constructs to understand when examining the Kemetic way of life is that of the importance of metaphor. If you fail to understand the Kemetic use of metaphor in constructing their philosophical "house," you will draw inaccurate conclusions about that house.

This failure of understanding can particularly affect our interpretation of the Kingship in Ancient Africa. The Divine Kingship was integral to the Kemetic way of life and has been sorely misinterpreted over the years. As we shall see upon closer examination, the Pharaoh, or King, was not *the* God. In the Kemetic system, he was God's representative on earth and was expected to serve as the penultimate example of a life lived according to God's principles, with ever-increasing identification with consciousness of God.

The Spiritual Universe and God

European thinkers are primarily empiricists. That is, they tend to make judgements and classify things, people, and events according to their five senses. As we address the "divine kingship," we must keep in mind that African people have always conceived of the world as a spiritual entity. Africans have always assumed that the essence of reality was not in what could be seen. That which could be seen, touched, tasted, felt, or smelled was no more than an incomplete reflection of an essentially spiritual reality. Observable phenomena were only representations and symbols. One needed both the brain and the heart to fully appreciate reality.

When non-Africans, then, tried to appreciate the magnitude of the African cosmology (the Kemetic structure of the world), they always found themselves confused and overwhelmed by its "complexity" and apparent "contradictions."

Recently, the Japanese thought that they knew how the Great Pyramid had been constructed. They thought that it was a simple method of "technology" and assumed that their technology was superior to that of the Ancient Kemites. That might in fact be true for microchips and automobiles. But integral to an understanding of the building of the pyramids is an understanding of what it takes to build the human spirit. It was "psychology," not technology, that built the pyramids. It was the knowledge of mind, not just the knowledge of matter. Only when non-African people understand what it takes to build the human spirit will they be able to replicate those mighty structures, which are a testimony to the union of spirit, soul, intelligence, energy, and matter.

So, we are looking with the wrong eyes--empirical eyes. If we look with the eye that transcends the senses, we can begin to see a system of thought whose elements are consistent and harmonious with spiritual principles.

African View of God

In order to understand the notion of Divine Kingship, we must first understand what the Africans believed about God. God was not an entity that started a process and then left it to manage on its own. He did not sit around in His white robe and in His white skin and arbitrarily dictate the fate of certain select (chosen) people. He was not a God who would occasionally intervene in creation, dropping in when He was solicited and going out when He was ignored. Instead, He was integrated into every fiber of reality, time, and space.

African people understood that from the high to the low there was God. They looked to the sky and saw God. They looked at the earth and saw God. They looked at the jackal, the lion, even the buzzard and the vulture and saw God.

This is not polytheism. In their pure and highest belief, the Ancient Kemites were not a polytheistic people. They simply recognized that God is vast and that He informs and unifies all of creation. The so-called "gods" were not themselves God, but simply reflected certain aspects of God's principles, ways, and consciousness.

Heru (Horus),[12] who was the holder of the earth and the vanquisher, ruled the domain of the "living." Ausir, the father of Heru and the savior of man, the one who was crucified and resurrected, ruled the domain over the "dead." God rules over both the living and the dead. The whole concept of the Resurrection shows that there is no such thing as oblivious, unconscious death. God can make death become life, even though it cannot be seen with the naked eye.

In the same way, Heru is a manifestation of his father Ausir who lives in him. The father and son were separate, but one. The dead father was alive in the living son, and the living son was potentially alive in the form of his father.

Contradictory? Not if you understand the holistic nature of African reality. Africans and other non-Europeans hold the belief that their ancestors are, in a spiritual sense, "alive" and at work in their descendants' lives. This strand of thought runs through virtually all of the major religions. We can even see it in science, where the genetic "explorers" have found that we inherit many of our physical and even our psychological characteristics.

God is particular and universal. He is specific and general. He is found in one space at one time in one manifestation, but He is simultaneously found in all manifestations. He is male and female. He is the sun and the moon, the light and the darkness. Because He is all things, nothing contradicts His presence. He unifies the dichotomies of this world manifested in His oneness.

We must appreciate that unity exists in the face of apparent paradox in order to systematically understand and appreciate Kemetic theology. If we do not understand the philosophy behind the theology, we will distort its interpretation.

When Europeans came into contact with our ancestors, they called them "polytheistic idolaters" who did not appreciate the essence and the substance of the one God. The irony is that Africa gave the world monotheism! People who came into Africa observed the devoted activities of people who saw in all of these manifestations the Divine Manifestation. They said that African people were pagans who worshipped everything and anything. But the Africans of these ancient times were expressing in visual and illustrative terms concepts which the outsiders could not see. They believed that there was a parallel force shining in the spiritual world that was responsible for all life in the spiritual realm, in the same way that the sun ruled in the physical realm. The sun was simply a metaphor. They understood that the *invisible* was pre-eminent, the producer of the visible. The *visible* merely instructs us about the form of the invisible.

The tragic distortions of Western interpretations of African thought are indicative of a failure to understand the significance of metaphor and the vitality of wholism. If you put your Western "logic cap" on, you will get lost.

Ancient African Kingship

With that background established, let us now move to examine the development of ancient African Kingship. In Ancient Kemet, the Pharaoh was the leader of the society, the person who was designated as the head of the body. The leader of the body manifested in his sphere the same God-like quality that we see in other aspects of the African cosmos.

For example, the sun was represented as Ra, Atum, loosely translated as "god." Certainly in the created world, the sun is the most powerful image and the most powerful manifestation of God. Ancient Kemites did not see the sun as *the* God; they saw the sun as "god," a manifestation of God's characteristics. The sun rules in its powerful, biochemical, electromagnetic, and physical capacity in a way that nothing else rules the physical observable universe. Everything in the physical world is totally dependent upon the sun. It makes color, water, and even darkness since darkness is no more than the negation of the sun.

The Ancient Kemites had a sophisticated notion that said the sun came in the expression of the "eyes of Heru" and could be viewed in the "body of Nut." *(See Fig. 2)*. Nut was a metaphysical conception of an invisible entity whose body served as the vehicle through which the sun passed. They understood that something greater than the sun put the sun into being; but that in its domain, the sun was king.

The Kemites' Divine Kings, or "Pharaohs," were called by names that metaphorically related to the light. They could be called Sun (Ra), "Son of Ra," "Heru," "Son of the Sun," or "Son of the Light." King Rameses the Great was called all of these names. Just as the sun ruled within its sphere, so did the Kemetic kings. They ruled within the sphere of the cosmos of social/human/cultural interaction. They ruled the world of government, within the sphere of the spirit and the intellect.

In his sphere, the Pharaoh was "god." Not *the* God, but "god." In his realm, he was to symbolize and epitomize the best of human possibility. He thus had tremendous responsibility. He had to offer an example of compliance and commitment to truth, of exemplary moral conduct, and he had to foster unity in the kingdom. With the same fervor that people were expected to govern their own minds and bodies, the Pharaoh was expected to govern the land. Kemet then became a macrocosm, the larger example, of each person's responsibility to rule and discipline their own human spirit.

As long as Pharaoh understood that he was "god" and not *the* God, he was in good shape. Unfortunately, some kings reckoned themselves to be *the* God. These kings literally lost their sanity: They forgot the limits of their appointment and their responsibility to serve *the* God and the people.

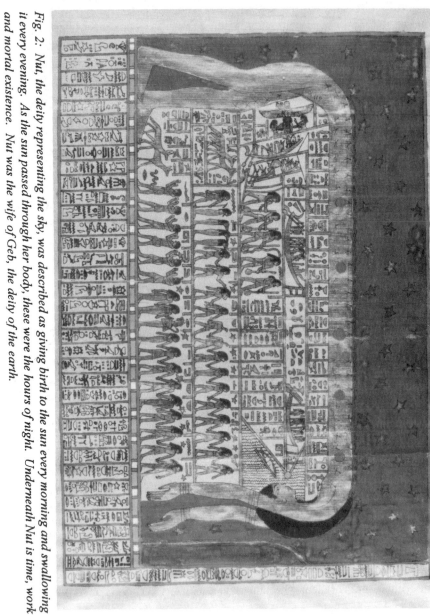

Fig. 2: Nut, the deity representing the sky, was described as giving birth to the sun every morning and swallowing it every evening. As the sun passed through her body, these were the hours of night. Underneath Nut is time, work and mortal existence. Nut was the wife of Geb, the deity of the earth.

The prophets and priests who had a vision of the truth objected to kings who lost sight of this mission. They recognized that God was the Creator of all things and was manifested in all things. They understood the dangers inherent in sliding from the idea that "God is everywhere" into the error of saying that "Everything is God." The prophets Muhammed, Abraham, Moses, Noah, even Jesus and the others consistently objected when the people began to elevate the manifestation of God to the form of being the God.

The process of establishing proper leadership included a highly developed system of initiation rituals and so-called "mystery schools." These rituals and educational institutions taught people how to cultivate their own leadership. They taught budding leaders how to rule their persons the way Pharaoh ruled the kingdom.

In our being, we have a variety of organs, muscles, and bones. We have appetites, attitudes, and ideals. We have intelligence and emotions. Many times these states, provinces, or "gnomes[13]" conflict with each other and disrupt the unity of the kingdom. That is what happens when the head says one thing and the heart says another. Your personal Pharaoh then must step in and "unite the two lands."

Pharaoh, then, was to serve as the ultimate model for the process of growing towards unity and wholeness. He was the best example for rulership because his training for the position of Pharaoh and his cultivation into pharaonic leadership began before birth. The Pharaoh did not assume that high office by getting elected. He did not use campaign slogans and public relations techniques. He was Pharaoh before he was born. This is how it happened: The wisest elders in the land, the pharaonic teachers, would determine when a Pharaoh was in line to be born. They believed that he would be molded in the womb and cultivated by the ancestral spirits. Once he appeared, the wise teachers would educate him correctly.[14] He would receive his wisdom from those who understood the wisdom of the Ancients. He would learn of his lineage and of his development and functioning as a human being. He would be taught of the fullness of his responsibility, and be cultivated as the personification of the Divine Will of the people.

Functions of Pharaoh

What were some of the functions of the Pharaoh, the Divine King? How did the Divine King operate?

One thing is certain. He did not operate like our present-day world leaders. The President of the United States, and other leaders of modern-day nations, are not cultivated and prepared to assume their respective roles. They are merely custodians of power, manipulated by power-holders. They are not systematically educated from before birth to genuinely understand who they are. They are not systematically taught how to align their will with the Divine Will. They do not necessarily learn of their unique relationship with the Ruler of the universe. They often fail to understand that they are but vessels through which *the* God may elect to manifest Himself. Presidents and contemporary leaders today must simply win popularity contests. Their selection is guided neither by principles nor values of human excellence, but by the ability to wield and manipulate power.

Pharaoh, on the other hand, was expected to authenticate his leadership through the benefits that accrued to the people because of his leadership. These benefits were not necessarily material ones, but benefits that embraced the highest possibilities of peace, productivity and happiness for the people. People do not work well if they are not living well or thinking well. On that basis, the Kemetic kingdom was able to thrive for many years. Its citizens did not need to exploit human beings to build or maintain the social order or the magnificent physical structures. They were able to cultivate citizens and workers who had discipline, skill, and commitment.

In looking at the functions of the Divine King, we note the responsibility to "unite the two lands." To briefly give some background, there was an "Upper Kemet," which encompassed the southern region of (what is now Egypt), and "Lower Kemet," which comprised the northern region. Upper Kemet was represented by a white conical crown and Lower Egypt by a red oval crown. The Pharaoh wore the two crowns on his head to denote the unity of the two kingdoms.

There is much powerful imagery here. The conical and oval crowns speak to the power of the strength of procreation. They speak to the importance of cultivating life. They utilize one of the most distinct images of the Creator by symbolizing the creative energy of the life processes.

When you bring together the energy of the "Upper" kingdom (the spiritual life) with the energy of the "Lower" kingdom (material and technological capacity and knowledge), you can then generate a new creative life form. The uniting of Upper and Lower Kemet unleashed powerful creative energy. It resulted in tremendous advances in cultural and technical life, including the building of pyramids and temples and the forming of some of the largest universities that have ever existed.

Ancient Kemetic science also had "goddesses" who represented the strength of the South and the strength of the North. In the South, or Upper Kemet, there was the goddess Wajet, the cobra goddess. She represented vitality, concentration, precision, and deadliness. Her potent venom can instantly fell the largest animal. Her swaying, hypnotic, rhythm induces a trance-like state that makes it easier to make the final attack. Wajet represents the power of psychology and the suggestibility of the mind.

In the North, or Lower Kemet, the goddess is symbolized by the vulture. The vulture does not kill, but finds life in the dead. She can feed on the dead and so preserve her own life. She watches life transform into death, and then paradoxically transforms the energy of death to maintain life. She symbolizes immortality by displaying how life can come from death. She simultaneously demonstrates the transient nature of the material world and its ultimate transformation.

Unity of Good vs. Separation of Evil

Another aspect of the Pharaoh's work was to establish moral unity in the land. Not only did he work to unify the geography of Kemet under one political head, he was obligated to establish unity in the moral life.

The Biblical story of Satan or Lucifer ("Set" in the Kemetic story) says that he got kicked out of heaven, and in his isolation became the purveyor of evil. As long as "Set" is a disunited force, separated from good, he rules as a force of evil.

Evil, then, is the result of uncontrolled or disunited appetites. Good, holy (whole), divine appetites are those that work in conjunction with the life process. When those appetites are isolated, they are driven by their own self-interest, separated from service to the whole, and thereby become evil or demonic.

There is nothing wrong with eating. Eating too much is the problem. There is nothing wrong with sex. Uncontrolled sexual appetite is the problem. Defensive fighting preserves life; fighting for enjoyment is a broken, separated, evil activity when people engage in it as "sport" because it feels good to them. When killing becomes a sport, you know that Set is ruling.

Nothing is wrong with military power. But when military power becomes the primary objective, you know that the society is ruled by Set. A kingdom ruled by Set enjoys war. It has a military budget larger than any of its human service or development budgets. It builds more missiles than educational centers. There is greater pride in taking life than there is in preserving life.

Then there is Heru (called Horus), who we will discuss in the next sections of this book.[15] Kemetic science calls Heru the "god" of life. He moves around in the sky. You can see his work spread all over the heavens with the moon in one eye and the sun in the other eye. His falcon belly is speckled with the stars of the sky. Geb, the grandfather of Heru and the father of Set, gave Heru (through Ausir) rulership of the whole earth. Water, minerals, food, and all the riches that come out of the earth belong to Heru.

Heru was the good ruler of the Upper Kingdom; Set, his nemesis, was the evil ruler of the Lower Kingdom. In Kemetic science, the Pharaoh came to unite the two lands to bring Heru and Set to the place where they could hold hands. The Pharaoh stood over these opposites and, by his rulership of *will*, unified the manifestations of good and evil to create a union of powerful, productive, procreative peace.

In this process, the Pharaoh merged and transformed the powers of Set and the powers of Heru. Thus, Set was neutralized and was no longer evil. Heru's kingdom--Upper Egypt, analogous to the mental and psychological processes--was brought from the sky and established on earth. Set of the Lower Kingdom, analogous to the physical side of humanness, became the energy needed for irrigation, agricultural development, building temples, and feeding legitimate yet controlled human appetites.

Lesson for Today

These lessons, these analogies, are no less powerful as guide-lines. The leadership cannot be leaders unless they provide direction for the people and provide food for both the body and the spirit. Leaders must develop knowledge and vehicles by which the knowledge can be transmitted. We as people of African descent must have universities, publishing companies, libraries and museums--institutions that require money.

Is money evil? No! But disunited money is. Money that works in the service of "Set" is money wrongly used, broken away from the service of life. In the same way, we must judge religious, financial, political, and educational systems by how they are used. Are they operating as broken entities to feed uncontrolled appetites or are they operating in union with "Heru" by serving life? Are they able to unite the spiritual and the material? Do they bring together those two warring forces and unite them to produce and create? Those are the questions that must be answered.

We need economics. We must not shy away from that reality. We have to control capital. God gave us the resources of the earth. We must control some of the earth and develop ways to extract its resources and transform them into capital. Materialism is a problem only when there is brokenness and disunity, when the papyrus (symbol of material resources) is separated from the lotus (symbol of spiritual growth).

If you have only the papyrus, you have war technology but no moral balance. If you have only the lotus, you will not survive. You cannot eat meditation. You cannot drink prayer. You will only last so long without feeding your physical body.

We African Americans have a connection with our *own* South. Our leadership must understand that the "Lower Kingdom" of North America, the Caribbean, and South America must be united with the "Upper Kingdom" of the continent of Africa. We can become a potent force for our own development if we begin to study and understand Kemetic thought and its profound influence in society. We can become a potent force for our own development if we unite skills we have in the West with the resource-rich lands on the African continent.

We must understand the nature and power of "unity" and begin to work together in all of our communities. As rulers, leaders, thinkers, technologists, artists, laborers, we must be about building bridges. We must stop attacking each other because of ostensible differences. We cannot afford to alienate each other in that way. We must be able to see through the distortions used to divide us and recognize truth wherever it may be found.

We cannot afford to be broken. There is no "Black" or "African" liberation without liberation from the oppressive mind that fails to respect the dignity and unique power of women. There is no women's liberation that fails to appreciate their inseparability from men. We will not prosper as a people until we understand that African people of all faiths, from all walks of life and organizational affiliations, can work together to bring about a renewal and growth.

Slavery alienated us from the identification with God. We knew God and worshipped God, but we lost sight of the reality of God. This "reality" is that God works through men and the processes of his creation. Slavery convinced us that God only worked through others and "chose" other people. Slavery disrupted the interconnection between us and God. We must reconnect with the history of the past. We must understand that the past is manifested in the present and that yesterday and tomorrow meet here. Indeed, we are Pharaohs in the present who stand between the kingdom of the past and the kingdom of the future. As long as we choose Truth, we can receive the benefits the Creator has provided to those who follow His principles.

The ideas used to build the great societies of Africa's past are not forgotten by all her descendants. They are here with us now. We must reconnect with that truth and hold hands with each other. The explosion of that transformation will melt the enemy's bombs. They won't know what to do with us. The planes loaded with cocaine that make a beeline to our communities will crash. They won't be able to find another AIDS germ because we will have life in spite of them. They didn't give us life, so they can't take it.

We must begin to re-identify with God, knowing that there is a Light that lights every person who comes into the world. We must understand the powerful symbolism of Moses, who *freed* the people; of Noah who *gathered* the people; and Lot who *led* the people. We must appreciate the powerful symbolism of Jesus and Muhammed. We can be prophets, in a sense, ourselves, if we simply tell the truth. We don't have to look for God. He is looking for us!

Abu Simbel in Kemet at the mighty Colossus of Rameses has one wall in the lower portion where there were pictures of the Pharaoh fighting his enemies, gathering the food, writing and studying, and doing the things that people do in government and society. Up above his head were pictures of Heru, Ausir, Heteru (one of the regional deities of Upper Kemet), and Auset. The pictures depicted the spiritual mystery and drama of the confrontation between good and evil. The Heru-Set and Set-Ausir conflicts (and the ability of Auset to put the body of Ausir back together) immortalized the profound processes of life that have always gone on and find physical manifestation in the life of the Pharaoh. So above in the upper part of the wall, you see the god-picture metaphysically illustrated. Down below you see the "contemporary" story. You see how God manifested Himself in the developments and conflicts and the victories that Rameses encounters. Then, in the "holy of the holiest sanctuary of Abu Simbel," you find Ptah, the creator of the heavens and the earth and all of the Neters or forces of nature. Ptah was independent, conceived in the solitude of his own mind. Next to him sits his creations: Heru, Amon-Ra and the Pharaoh Rameses II.

The Pharaoh seems out of place. He was a physical being, while the others were spiritual. Why would he want to sit with them? Did he have an ego problem?

No, he did not. Perhaps he knew that if he carried God's authoritative utterance in his mouth, speaking the truth with confidence; that if he understood the world, people, and his responsibility; that if his life was devoted to manifesting justice; that if he influenced his people to awaken and rise as the water rises on the Nile, then he had a right to sit with the gods because the gods found their expression in him.

We must understand that the spiritual drama is a metaphor of life. God's presence is in all of our doing. The Divine Kingship is a manifestation of the highest understanding. The pharaonic symbol represents the potential of the human spirit. Slavery tore away the African American consciousness of the reality of God and our ability to "unite the kingdom."

We must begin to reunite inside and outside. We must begin to hold hands and love each other more than anything. Male and female must come together in heart as well as in body. The female principle of energy must merge with the masculine principle of energy, not only to procreate physical offspring, but new societies, new art, new science, and new understanding. We must develop the eye of understanding, and open it so that light can come down to the darkest chamber. We must understand that we can be free *now*.

IV

THE MYTH OF AUSIR
AND BLACK AWAKENING

"Awaken and rise up. The dead depart this earth as dead people, but they leave it as if they were alive. The link is unloosed. The knot is untied. I cross this portal. I have thrown to the ground all evil which is on me. They go towards Ausir. Their faces find a new life and strength." (From The Book of Coming Forth by Day [Budge, 1973], *Auset and Heru are speaking: "The Awakening").*

We have lost an appreciation for the power of the myth. Our ancient people in Africa for thousands and thousands of years contemplated the vastness of a universe that actually transcended description. They contemplated a reality and a greatness in the awesome reality of God and Nature that was beyond the ability to grasp and describe in words. The brilliant minds of those people pursued science as far as it could take them. They finally found that science ran out. They took theology and philosophy as far as they could take them, and they found out that all logic ran out. They said, "If we can't put these descriptions into reality, let's see if our descriptions can transcend reality." They found that time and logic occupied space and time, but what they were trying to describe transcended time and space. They had to go beyond what was mere description, although the description alluded to the vastness and although the science pointed to the Infinite. They were unable to be totally descriptive of this transcendent reality that was known as "the Infinite."

Understanding Mythology

In our Euro-American education we have been taught that mythology has to do with such things as "Paul Bunyan," "Rumpelstiltskin," "Sleeping Beauty," and these kinds of fairy tales. The mythology of the ancient Africans, however, described a reality that was too big to fit into time and space.

If the myth is a key to a higher reality, then in order to more fully rediscover ourselves and awaken the other (third) eye, we need to understand this key. (By the way, the two physical eyes see the physical world and the "third eye" sees the non-physical reality). In order to awaken the third eye, it is necessary to rediscover the power of the myth.

In this chapter, we are going to touch on something of what our ancient ancestors have taught us through their mythology. It is very interesting because the ones who preceded us understood that their responsibility was not to their time alone. They understood that their responsibility was to eons yet unborn. They understood that the message of truth which they pursued was not a message just for that time and that place, but it had to be a message for all times and all places. The messages left coded in myths and symbols are timeless. The Truth which they described is a permanent Truth. All we need to do if we want to understand truth is to go back and pick up the codes that the Ancients left us in the past and we can better understand our circumstances in the present.

The Myth of Ausir

Ausir (Osiris), according to the ancient Kemetic myth, was of divine origin. He came out of heaven and dwelt among men. Ausir was the first one who taught civilization and cultivation (how to go about bringing life out of the earth). Ausir was the first teacher of worship of the Gods.[16] Ausir taught science and religion because there was no distinction between the two in Ancient Kemet. Since he understood both the mundane and the celestial, he was able to bring both worlds together. Therefore, he was "of heaven and of earth."

The Myth of Ausir
and Black Awakening

All mythologies describe the movement or evolution of life from the plane of unity or oneness (the spiritual world) to the plane of duality (the physical world). Therefore, in this story, we find that Ausir had a twin brother whose name was Set. Set (who later became "Satan", "Shaitan" or "Devil") was guided by a contrasting nature that compelled him to attack this scientific truth-bringer called Ausir. Set wanted to slay or destroy Ausir because Set represented the personification of evil and destructiveness which eats away at order, justice, righteousness, and ultimately at Truth. Set was the natural opposing force to "good."

The ultimate enemy to Truth is falsehood or deception. Truth, like energy, can neither be created nor destroyed. The story tells us that Ausir was tricked into the loss of his power. Set had a party and called together his 72 co-conspirators. He built a chest (casket) that was perfect to fit the size of Ausir. Everyone at the party was invited to try to fit into the chest and Ausir was the last to try. The chest had been custom-made for Ausir, so when he got into it, he fit perfectly. The co-conspirators closed the chest, sealed him in it, threw it into the river, and the river took the chest out to the sea. It was eventually consumed by a mighty tree that encircled the chest and grew up around it. The tree was such a beautiful tree that a king in a strange land took the tree to his land and built his castle around the tree that was actually the tomb of Ausir.

In this brief summary of the Ausirian myth, we now meet Auset (Isis), the spirit of truth, comfort, diligence, perseverance, and determination. Auset represents the ever-continuing resilience and regeneration of human nature. When Auset goes in search of Ausir, we are told that she finds the tree with the chest and reclaims the body. But, evil Set (who is always lurking in the dark) recognizes that Auset has taken away Ausir's body. Set manages to find the body. He said, "This time I will get rid of Ausir (the vessel of goodness) once and for all. I will mutilate him." The myth continues and Set then cuts up the body of Ausir into fourteen pieces and throws the dismembered parts away into the river.

But, the persistent, resilient, determined, human spirit, represented by Auset, reappears. With perseverance and persistence, she finds all of the dismembered pieces of Ausir except for the phallus which was swallowed up by a fish. Tehuti (Thoth) in cooperation with Auset was able to restore the dead Ausir to life. We are told that Ausir (Osiris) was resurrected from the dead, ascended into heaven and became the judge of the departed souls. These are the essential elements of one of several versions of this very old and complex myth.

The Contemporary Relevance of the Myth

If the Ancients were talking about that time, prior time and subsequent time, we should be able to find in this myth which has persisted for over 6,000 years in various forms, some message for us in this day and time. People could not have believed this story for such a long time with such devotion unless it spoke to something that was universally present in all eras of history.

We believe that the ancient Africans were telling us something about today. The images from the myth suggest a striking parallel to a story from contemporary history. A group of people went to a "party" about 400 years ago. At the party they were tricked and locked into the bottom of a chest (or a ship). They went to this party because of their respect for some foreigners who had come to their land. They saw the foreigners as fellow human beings (Brothers). They did not know that these different human beings were driven by a force to conquer and control. With the trusting nature of Ausir they listened to the deceptive invitation: "Just come with us and we can take you to a great new world." The co-conspirators from England, Portugal, Holland, France, and from all parts of Europe got together and enslaved poor Ausir, the one who had brought civilization, religion, science, all of the great gifts of culture to the world. They sealed Ausir in the bottom of the ship (coffin), dropped him into the river (call it the Niger River or some other African waterway), and sent it toward the sea. This group of people, represented as Ausir, eventually found themselves consumed in a mighty tree which trapped the chest and grew up around it.

This image suggests the next step in the process whereby the tomb of Ausir finds itself "in the house of a king in a strange land." Let's suggest that the tree was Anglo-American culture and the house was the new European land called "America." The co-conspirators took the chest that contained the patriarch of civilized life and used it as the main pillar in their new house.

In this image, we see Ausir descend from life and high accomplishment to a state of death and hopelessness. We see Ausir tricked into imprisonment, transported across the sea, consumed in a culture (tree), and established as the main pillar in the house of a strange king. So far, the images of the myth closely parallel the history of the African enslavement. If the story parallels the captivity, does it also offer a resolution? We need to find an Auset.

If the myth is correct, Auset should be (here) somewhere. Sure enough, we find Auset in the history. Auset comes in the form of Marcus Garvey, Elijah Muhammad, Harriett Tubman, and Noble Drew Ali. Their lives' mission was a persisting search for the body of Ausir. "Where is the one who has been slain? He doesn't know who he is because he is dead. He has been killed by being tricked out of his native reality, culture, and consciousness. He has been entombed in the tree of an alien culture which maintains his state of death." These images of Auset represent the perseverance, the determination, the resilience of the African soul seeking itself. This perseverance took the form of teaching and working to bring the people messages that would free them from the foreign "tree" and their coffin, and would ultimately revive their lives.

Who is Set?

It is important to understand Set's identity because he was operating in opposition to the life that was being established by Ausir. Set represented the personification of evil or the negative force in life. Set was the force whose objective was to overwhelm and destroy the divine life that was in Ausir. Once the body had been taken, sealed, and floated away, Set should have been satisfied. Set, however, was aware of the resilience within the Divine life. He knew that he had to persist in his efforts to destroy that special life that could be subdued, but not really killed. Set engaged in mutilation of the body in order to impede the progress of its resurrection. It was not enough that the body of Ausir had been kidnapped, robbed of its culture, and robbed of its life (i.e., its consciousness). The mutilation was done in order to fragment the vessel which contained the life of Ausir. Dispersing the pieces was intended by Set to thwart resurrection.

This mutilation was activated against modern day Ausir by Set's break-up of families. He systematically disrupted the natural alliance between male and female. He began to feed in ideas that made it difficult for males and females to work together and to raise families together. He worked to break up the African extended family which served to bring together the entire community. He bred disrespect between the men and women by using the men for studs and women for breeders. The notion that you really didn't need a family system was an idea established by Set.

The Ausirian spirit became confused because of the mutilation that was taking place. The people began to believe Set's lies. The women began to say to the men, "I don't need you. I can do for myself." The men began to say to the women, "There are so many women around here, Sister, if you don't want me, I'll find ten others to replace you." The sense of responsibility and the alliance that existed between the two became something that was severed by Set because he understood that the body had to be mutilated or it might come back to life.

Then, Set proposed: "Let's try to thoroughly disrupt their commonality. Let's divide the people politically." Set began to mix them up into all kinds of strange camps. "Let's make some of them Democrats. Let's make some of them Republicans. Let's make some of them Rastafarai. Let's make some of them Nationalists and some of them Socialists. Let's get them very confused about who they are and let them believe that their membership is what they really are. Set was determined to mutilate Ausir so that he would begin to lose sight of his natural unity and common objectiveness. "We will encourage them to be Methodists and Baptists of all descriptions: A.M.E., C.M.E., A.M.E. Zion, Missionary Baptist. We will sprinkle some of them, baptize others and anoint others. It was Auset who kept reminding Ausir: "None of this is you. You are really one who seeks submission to God and finds peace by submitting yourself to the oneness of the order of nature and bringing yourself into alliance with that oneness. That's your true nature. You share a common destiny with all of yourself."

All of these divisions were engineered by Set, who understood that Ausir worked as a single body moving in a single direction, held together by a single principle: **"Oneness."**

Another mutilation is that of economic divisiveness: the belief that individual hoarding will produce wealth. The failure of the people to cooperate with each other in economic development has kept the body economically mutilated. Individual wealth is never genuine wealth because it must rely on others to grow and it must serve others to be sustained. The body must work together in order to develop economic power for the body. We can never do this so long as we feel that wealth is an individual matter. Set had fragmented the body so that the mutilated Ausir would only bring ever-increasing wealth to Set and poverty to himself.

Then there is the spiritual division that makes it difficult for us to understand that spirituality is bigger than religion. It is the kind of division that makes it difficult to understand that reason and spirituality are not at odds with each other. Reason augments spiritual truth; emotion augments rational truth; and the combination works to produce the spiritual vision. The spiritual division has us working on the parts. Now what are the parts? We have one group over here that says: "If you feel anything or show any emotion, then you are not being religious. It's got to be completely rational with no feeling." Some religious groups have become so "rational" that if you aren't literate, you can't attend their church. You have to be able to read and read well. These same people who are rational and literate can't imagine being spontaneous. Then you go to some other churches and they knock over the benches, kick over the piano, beat you across the head, and throw their pocketbooks. If you can't show spontaneous emotion then your sincerity is doubted. The division requires that you should be either rational or emotional.

Then there are the fundamentalists who accept the literal meaning of what they find in their religious books. They believe that the book is literally "God's Word" and it cannot be questioned, even when it conflicts with common sense. These are people who have spiritually divided themselves because their feelings and faith are telling them one thing and their reason is telling them another.

Then there is the spiritual and internal division that is created by the representation of God as a Caucasian image. The child growing up under the influence of this image fails to see a natural relationship between himself/herself and God. The consequence is a person who has a strong faith in the reality and power of God but associates that God with an image completely different from himself. This creates a split in the personality and causes Africans to believe in the power of people other than themselves. This creates the need to see one's Black self in contrast to the white image of power, purity, and greatness. So the Black self becomes evil, dirty, and powerless in contrast to the white image of power and goodness.

Set has caused a familial division, political division, spiritual division, fraternal division, community division, but worst of all is the division against the self. The degree to which we have been programmed and engineered to behave in opposition to ourselves is the worst mutilation. This is the mutilation that took the head from the body. Paolo Freire[17] has observed: "The most potent weapon of the oppressor is the mind of the oppressed." Once the head has been taken from the body, even the process of resurrection is resisted. The loss of the head represents the ultimate destruction of the human.[18]

There is considerable evidence of the consequence of removing the head. The second major cause of death among African American men under the age of thirty-five is homicide. Ninety percent of those who commit these murders are other African American men. We engage in a variety of forms of self-murder because we have been infused with the mind of self-destruction. We die of lung cancer 25% more frequently than Euro-Americans. Lung cancer is the most preventable form of cancer. Why don't we prevent it? We won't stop smoking. They give us poison, label it as poison, but because our heads are severed, we take the poison with great happiness and enthusiasm. They give us intoxicants, call it "toxic" (which literally means poison), and we proceed to take the poison. They tell us that if we continue to eat excessive amounts of salt and pork, our days will be numbered. Despite this warning, we won't stop eating those ribs or chitterlings.

We have the facts that cardiovascular diseases and strokes are seven times more likely to cause death if you are an African American. Prostate cancer and cervical cancer, the most curable forms of cancer, are the greatest cause of death. Cervical cancer is 25% higher among African American women. Prostate cancer is three times higher among African American men. Why? Primarily because of the unavailability and the unwillingness to get health care. The doctor says that something is wrong with you and you don't want to believe it until it's too late; until the pain gets so bad you can't do anything about it. We ignore the warning signs because the head has been severed from the body. This happens because we are intellectually divided - the Ausirian mutilation has split us away from knowledge that we can use for ourselves.

The Resurrection of Ausir

What happens in the resurrection? They tell us in the Ausirian story (myth) that the resurrection requires the opening of the mouth; the opening of the eyes; and the opening of the ears. We are told that Auset went to Tehuti. Tehuti is referred to as the scribe of the Neters. Tehuti is also the term out of which the word "thought" emerged. Tehuti personifies the thinking process. We are told that Auset, with perseverance, persistence, determination, and resilience, went to Tehuti and got the message to bring to Ausir which would begin to take the chilled mutilated body and to resurrect him into the Sakhu (which is the divine spiritual body). He would then be transformed for the resurrection in one unified form.

In the ancient Kemetic language, to be "deaf" meant that you were deaf, dumb, and blind. That's why the words "death" and "deaf" are so close in spelling. To be deaf is like being dead. Hearing is the symbol of consciousness. It is open perceptiveness, the openness to receive without barriers. You can close your eyes and you can close your nose and you can hold your breath, but you can still hear. The ears are always open. They represent consciousness, awareness, absorbing things to bring about recognition. Things can be heard even before they get to you. You can hear behind you when you can't see behind you. You can hear what you can't feel. You can hear what you can't smell. So the ears represent the symbol of consciousness. In order to bring life back into the body of Ausir, Auset had to go through the ritual words, messages and acts given to her by Tehuti.

The myth has much meaning. There were specific rituals to be followed in order to restore consciousness (hearing to the dead). Vision was restored through the ritual of opening of the eyes. The process of restoring vision is illustrated in another part of the epic when Heru (Horus) has a battle with Set. Heru, the son of Ausir, went into battle against his uncle Set. During the battle, Set put out one of Heru's eyes and Heru in turn took Set's testicles. Auset, the mother of Heru, went back to Tehuti and said, "What do we need in order to restore the vision to the eyes?" Tehuti told Auset that she could restore Heru's sight by putting spittle in his eyes. The spittle represents the substance of the mouth. The mouth is the mechanism for the expression of ideas and the expression of thought. This part of the myth tells us that it is the "word" that emerges from the mouth. By taking the spittle (the expression from the mouth) and rubbing it into the eye-vision can be restored.

Vision is the pool into which all the senses pour. Vision tells us not only what is, but what can be. Vision not only reflects images of what exists, it also creates images of what can be. The "third eye" is the eye of prophetic or creative vision because the physical eyes simply reflect what already exists in the created or material world. The eye of higher vision shows what has always been and what can be. In order to restore vision, the dead must be given words of Truth. This expression "spittle from the mouth of Truth" restores vision.

Finally, Auset's ritual to resurrect Ausir required the opening of the mouth. This is a very important ritual that has found continuing expression in the Catholic church in the administration of Holy Communion. The communicant is given "the blood and the body" of Christ in the mouth. In opening the mouth, the dead is given the ability to speak, and with "the word," everything that is named is called to life. *The Bible* says, "In the beginning was the word." Adam, in the *Holy Qur'an*, was taught the "names" of things.[19] His ability to identify the name or essence of things in creation gave him the power over creation. This is the power of science given to man to know and exercise control over things in nature. The "word" was the source of power which permitted man to transform, change, and master what existed in "the Garden." By hearing Truth, consciousness (hearing) is restored to the dead. Given the inspiration that restores vision (opens the eye), the resurrected is able to speak the word of Truth. The resurrected Ausir becomes a creative scientist and builder.

In translation, this means that in order to be resurrected, the dead must be restored to consciousness and proper form, culture or thought. The members of the mutilated body must be reconnected. The Spirit of Auset must be among us and we must respond to her efforts. We must listen to the instruction of thought and reason as it comes from Tehuti. The secret of resurrection was stored in this myth for thousands of years in order to be reassembled to restore African people to life. The battle between Ausir and Set is a perpetually reoccurring cycle throughout time. True to prophecy, Ausir, Auset, and Set seem to know their roles and play them appropriately to the drama. At this cycle in history, we are the mutilated Ausir and our oppressors have assumed the role of Set. The ritual for the revival of consciousness is done by providing stimulating educational experiences that teach people the nature of themselves to get them to awaken from the sleeping awareness that is lying dormant waiting to be restored to power. We must be prepared to revive the mind that laid the foundation for the mightiest man-made structures that have existed in the world. We must restore the mathematical insight that our people were able to gain from the study of the heavens. We must restore our understanding of the processes and transformations of nature, appreciating its relationship to ourselves. We must be able to bring the word of Truth to revive our dormant consciousness. The human consciousness cannot die. The mind does not die. Truth does not fail. Truth is what is, always has been and always will be. The only way that you can control consciousness is by putting it to sleep.

The "eye," the vision, needs to be restored. We must, once again, learn to see beyond what's visible to the physical eyes. We have got to have the spittle of Truth rubbed into our eyes. This spittle comes from Tehuti: the words of Marcus Garvey or Elijah Muhammed that gave new life to (Malcolm X) al Hajj Malik Shabazz, and thousands of others. There were thousands of unconscious people restored to life by the "spittle" that came from Elijah or Marcus. These thousands of African people were spit on by Auset and they began to rotate in a restored consciousness that was their true self. The "spittle" or the word came to tell us who we are, where we came from, what our potential is, and it gave us a vision! This vision is one of leadership. It is not a dream of followership. As we have discovered, the dream of followership has done little to substantially change our condition. We must follow our true identity and the leadership that respects that identity. We must then build institutions which enhance and secure that identity.

The story of Ausir lets us know that Set is a continuous part of our existence. He takes many forms, but he keeps returning. Set is going to be here, so we must learn to deal with him. In order to deal with Set, Ausir must know his true identity. Auset must also know her true identity.

This identity must be rooted in an authentic history, a collective commitment and a bold and courageous vision. We want to develop a vision of our own schools in America that build upon the resources of our people, our time, our reality. We want textbooks coming out of our publishing companies that can be circulated around the world to let all people know the reality of who we are. The vision must be one of our own educational institutions that will produce scholars who engage in intellectual development and provide insight into the resolution of the many problems that confront us. The vision must be for constructive artistic and not barbaric artistic indulgence.

What Will our Legacy Be?

We must seriously address the question of what will our legacy be? Will we leave the strong spirit of a Harriet Tubman or Fannie Lou Hamer? Will we leave the institution-building vision of Mary McLeod Bethune? Will we leave the bold courage of Adam Clayton Powell, Paul Robeson, or Martin Luther King, Jr? We need a vision that can make us see what is not, but what can be. We must see ourselves as world class manufacturers, bankers, traders, while maintaining the highest values of Maat: Truth, justice, righteousness, and harmony. We must work to give our children a legacy at least equal to what has been given to us. If we do not, those ancestors who made it possible for us to be here will meet us at the gate of our transformation and will turn their backs to us. Our hearts will be put on the scale of justice and weighed by the Anubis, balanced by the feather of Maat. *(See Fig. 3)*. Only the heart that has been lightened by its efforts to establish the values of Maat will find balance by Maat. The *Holy Qur'an* says, ''The balance that day will be true (to a nicety); Those whose scale (of good) will be heavy, will prosper; Those whose scale will be light, will find their souls in perdition, for that they wrongfully treated our sins'' (VII:8,9). If our contribution has not been respectable, then we will be turned away from the portals of the sanctuary of Ausir and we will be judged unworthy of transformation into that higher form. We will not get into the Elysian fields and play on the grounds of universal growth and rejuvination, where our ancestors

Fig. 3: The judgement scene of weighing the heart of the deceased. At the left, Anubis (with the dog head), leads in the deceased. A second figure of Anubis checks the balance while Tehuti (Thoth) records the results. The "Eater" stands ready to take the deceased if balance is not achieved. Then Heru presents the deceased to Ausir in front of whom emerges a lotus on which stands the four "Sons of Heru"; behind are Isis and Nephthys. Notice the double crown worn by Ausir.

already reside. They paid the price. That's why we are here.

Our ancient African ancestors teach us that resurrection requires that the mouth must be opened along with the ears. The eye must be restored, and "the words" must be given to the deceased. The "words" are the proper names of things. What are these proper names? The ancient African concept of the "Neters" is one example of "proper names." The "Neters" is a name. The Neters represent the laws of nature. *The Holy Qur'an* teaches us that all of the universe is laid out as a classroom to study, as a book. We are told that by studying the principles of nature (Neters) outside (exoteric) and in our own nature (esoteric), we can begin to come into the awareness and the consciousness of what we need to transform the world. There are principles of child development that can be learned from observing the bee. There are principles of human productivity that can be learned by studying the ant. Principles of social organization can be seen in the workings of a flock of birds. Principles of child care and mothering can be found with baboons, monkeys, dogs, cows and cats. Principles of economic development can be found in the division of labor that exists in the beehive. You can begin to understand the need for organization and leadership by looking at the cosmic order. You can begin to understand the principles of mathematical precision and order which refute the notion of disorder. You can begin to find that in diversity there is unity. Individuality exists only to complement the individuality of everybody else. It means nothing unless it is working in the cooperative body. These principles can be learned without reading a published book or sitting in any school classroom, but with what the Creator has already given - the universal textbooks.

We discover that Truth is universal and that all new discoveries simply confirm old ones. This makes us realize that what is to be known is already known. Oriental wisdom speaks of the "Akashic records" which are recorded in the collective unconscious of all people. These records contain the essence of human learning through all times. Though not specific in content, they contain the essence and processes of all universal wisdom. The Akashic records lay open volumes and volumes of tens of thousands of years of ancient human history. These records are working right now in our minds. One of the challenges of the authentic African psychologists is to rediscover how to unlock the Akashic records that we have. We can then begin to transform ourselves so that we can be restored to our former selves.

"*My name does not pass away. I am the soul that created the deep, that makes its seat in God's domain. My nest, my place of birth, is hidden and my eggs have not been broken. I am lord of the heights and I have made my nest in the sky but I come down to earth that I may do away with my uncleanliness. Oh Lord, Ausir, come then and establish me and make me strong. Grant that I may enter the land of everlastingness as you have done along with your father Ra, whose body never passed away and who is one who indeed does not die. I have not done that which you hate but have praised your name among those who love your divine essence. May your spirit love me and not reject me and may you not let my body decay but deliver me as you did deliver yourself. Let life rise out of death. Let not decay make an end of me or my enemies come against me in their many forms. I am the great one, the son of a great one. I am the fiery one, the son of the fiery one whose head was restored to him after it had been cut off. The head of Ausir, the risen savior, is not to be taken from him and my head shall not be taken from me. I have risen up and knitted myself together. I have made myself whole. I renew myself and grow young again. I am one with Ausir, Lord of eternity.*" (From **The Book of Coming Forth By Day** as translated by Maulana Karenga in **Selections from the Husia**).

CONCLUSION

This discussion has focused upon just one aspect of a multifac-
eted and complex system which describes the human psyche according to
ancient Kemetic tradition. As we cautioned from the outset, the entirety
of the Kemetic cosmology is actually a comprehensive description of the
psyche of man. To separate out a mono-disciplinarian approach to the
study of the mind does an injustice to this complex system.

The amazingly complex theology of Ancient Kemet represents a
series of allegories which define the workings of nature and, most
importantly, the genesis and potentialities of man. These myths and
symbols transcend the empirical conclusions of Western science and
describe man not only on the basis of what he does, but what he is.

We have chosen to look at the psychic components in a way that
the Ancients prescribed, because in that system we find a summary of
what a human being is. By implication, we can more effectively describe
the proper functioning of the human being and detect the deviations from
the African perspective. Each of these components of the seven-fold soul,
which we have described, has implications for understanding the nature
of the human being.

The fundamental conclusion about human nature, as implied by
the description of the Ba and the Atum, as well as the divine Ka, is that
the human being is transpersonal and essentially connected with the
divine and everything else in nature. There is a continuity in all that there
is, having its origin in the Creator.

These ideas of the African philosophy, the African cosmology,
are directly tied into the concepts of the ancient Kemetic personality.
Even though we may experience difficulty living within the "dome" by
which these ideas were transmitted, this kind of consciousness has
remained among African people. This is in contrast to the dualistic and
materialistic conception of the Euro-American psychologist who would
be appalled at even admitting that "psyche" once meant soul--even to
them.

The Ka, on the other hand, brings balance to the picture of the
human being. Ka shows that the human being is not only of heavenly
material, but also of earthly material. Let us not assume for a minute that

the Ancients did not envision a wholistic picture. They understood that you have got to live on earth, but they also understood that earth was, and is, transitory.

Intelligence is viewed as being multiple in its dimensions-- rational, spiritual, and ethical. The intelligent person is not simply one who has mastered a set of techniques, but one who is prudent enough to know when and how to apply these techniques. The intelligent one is certainly not one who attempts to perform independently of his moral and spiritual obligation to the Creator and the rest of humanity. The Akhu and the Putah provide a perception of intelligence which require self-mastery and service to one's higher self.

Today we must reconnect with the truth taught by the Ancient Kemites with this *Light from Ancient Africa*. The human being will ultimately recapture the entirety of what he has been since his inception: a divine form ready to reunite with its divine genesis. Through realization of one of Ancient Kemet's most consistent motifs, *transformation*, we can transform the raw material of our transient form, to the higher being from which we sprang.

Our psychological problems are ultimately resolved by the redemption of knowledge of our self (e.g., soul). It is the only knowledge that frees us. In the coffin text of Ancient Kemet, we find that the deceased pleads: "Don't take my soul (Ba). Do not detain my shade (Khaba). Open the path to my shade, my soul, and my intelligence (Akhu) to see the great God on the day of reckoning souls."[20]

Endnotes

1.Adapted from "Nile Valley Origins of Psychology" in Ivan Van Sertima's *Nile Valley Civilization*, J. of African Civilization, 1984.

2.We do acknowledge the work of certain European psychologist, such as Carl Jung, who postulated such concepts as the "collective unconscious" to the shame and the horror of his Euro-American scientific community. Such thinkers are considered deviants, radicals, and lacking credibility within their own ranks of Western scholarship.

3.This idea is discussed at greater length in Chapter III of this volume which discusses the ancient African concept of Divine Kingship.

4.Richard King (1990) in his book presents compelling evidence for this interpretation.

5.For a more detailed and comprehensive description of these qualities, the reader in search of broader knowledge and interpretation is encouraged to study the important text by Ra Un Nefer Ameen entitled *The Metu Neter.*

6.One conception of this idea which is retained in Christianity is the idea of the "Body Christ." (Galatians 3:24-29): You are all sons of God through faith in Christ Jesus, for all of you were baptized...).

7.The "Akashic record" is a concept from Buddhist metaphysics, which saw the mind of each person as a repository for all of the knowledge of the universe. Though an elusive potential, every human being properly developed could eventually access this infinite data base.

8.Maat is the ancient African concept which describes the force of truth, justice, righteousness, harmony and peace which is the functioning principle of entire creation.

9.The reader is encouraged to read *Chains and Images of Psychological Slavery* (Akbar, 1976).

10. We are aware that "Psyche" was a Greek goddess which served as the root of the term psychology. However, we know that the Greek gods and goddesses were based on the Kemetic Neters which symbolized human or natural processes.

11. The reader is encouraged to read the analysis of these functions of the self described in much greater detail in the writing of Ra Un Nefer Ameen's *Metu Neter.*

12. For the sake of consistency with popular usage, I will note the Greek designations of the Kemetic Neters, but for the sake of instruction, I will use the terminology from direct translation as offered by Ra Un Nefer Ameen from the ancient language of Kemet (See *Metu Neter*, Vol. I).

13. "Gnomes" was a term used by the Kemetic people to designate the various segments or divisions in the land.

14. This concept of the mission of the unborn finds its counterpart in the religious scriptures that prophesied the birth of a liberator or ruler in the time of Abraham, Moses, Jesus, and the unborn Messiah still awaited by some religious people. The idea finds root in the Kemetic cosmology.

15. See Section IV, entitled *The Myth of Ausir and Black Awakening.*

16. The worship of the "gods" for our people was a recognition of the neters. Neters does not mean gods. Neters means the forces of nature.

17. Paolo Freire (1975), *The Pedagogy of the Oppressed.*

18. According to tradition, Auset found the head of Ausir at Abydos, which became the highest shrine to Ausir in Ancient Kemet. This shrine became the place for pilgrimage of the devout from all over the land. The sacredness of this spot attests to the symbolic significance of relocating the head of Ausir.

19. "And he taught Adam all the names then presented them to the angels; He said: Tell me the names of those if you are right" (The *Holy Qur'an* II, 31).

20. *The Book of Coming Forth by Day* commonly *The Egyptian Book of the Dead.*

Bibliography

Akbar, N. *Chains and Images of Psychological Slavery*. Jersey City: New Mind Productions, 1984.

Ali, M.M. (trans.) The *Holy Qur'an*.

Ameen, R.U.N. *Metu Neter, Vol. 1*. Bronx, New York: Khamit Corporation, 1990.

Budge, E.A.W. *The Egyptian Book of the Dead*. New York: Dover Publications, 1967.

Freire, P. *Pedagogy of the Oppressed*. New York: Seabury Press, 1973.

James, G.G.M. *Stolen Legacy*. San Francisco: Julian Richardson Assoc., 1976.

Karenga, M. (trans.) *Selections from the Husia*. Los Angeles: Kawaida Publications, 1984.

King, R. *African Origin of Biological Psychiatry*. Germantown, Tennessee: Seymour-Smith, 1990.

Massey, G.M. *A Book of the Beginnings*, Vol. 1. Seacaucus, New Jersey: University Books, Inc., 1974.

Massey, G.M. *Gerald Massey's Lectures*. New York: Samuel Weiser, Inc., 1974.

Nobles, W.W. *African Psychology*. Oakland, California: Black Family Instiitute Publications, 1986.

Van Sertima, I. "Nile Valley Civilizations." *J. of African Civilizations*, 6(2), November 1984.

Acknowledgments

Even a small project like this requires the assistance of a rather considerable number of people.

Diane Reeder assisted early in the project with the rather tedious job of editing, which transposed these presentations from the spoken to the written word.

Rosalyn Nix, who is a regular employee of *Mind Productions*, is no doubt, the most important part of this project. She very aptly transcribed the lectures which were the source of these essays and did the entire layout for this book. We are very grateful to Roz because without her assistance and outstanding skills, this book would not have been possible.

Malcolm Aaron designed the cover with no more direction than a phone call and an inspiration. Thank you, Malcolm.

Abdul Shakir offered many forms of assistance and encouragement throughout this project and many other projects over the years, and I remain indebted to him for his assistance.

Byron Thomas, who is the orders manager for *Mind Productions*, must be acknowledged as well since he will be the one primarily responsible for the distribution of this and all of our materials

The person who coordinated the entire project, identifying the right people to do the right things at the right time and staying on me to finish this book, even when I had decided to forsake it, was my able assistant, Anwar Kwesi Diop. Anwar deserves my greatest appreciation for his persistent encouragement that I should put these ideas together in a written form. Thank you, Anwar, for your efforts on this project and all of the productive energy that you have brought to our work over the last four years. Neither this nor many other things would have been possible without your vigilant and creative solutions to problems of every form.

For those many unnamed people who have inspired and assisted me in so many ways for so many years, please accept my sincere gratitude.